TOM LANE

TESTED AND

MENTOR PLAYBOOK

FOR GROUP AND PERSONAL EXPERIENCE, OVERSIGHT, AND ACCOUNTABILITY

TOM LANE

TESTED AND

APPROVED

MENTOR PLAYBOOK

FOR GROUP AND PERSONAL EXPERIENCE, OVERSIGHT, AND ACCOUNTABILITY

GATEWAY®
PRESS

Tested and Approved: Mentor Playbook for Group and Personal Experience, Oversight, and Accountability

978-1-951227-68-5

ISBN: 978-1-951227-43-2 Mentor Playbook, companion guide to the resource book
Tested and Approved: 21 Lessons for Life and Ministry
ISBN: 978-1-951227-24-1 Hardcover
ISBN: 978-1-951227-25-8 eBook
ISBN: 978-1-64689-156-6 Audiobook

We hope you hear from the Holy Spirit and receive God's richest blessings from this book by Gateway Press. We want to provide the highest quality resources that take the messages, music, and media of Gateway Church to the world. For more information on other resources from Gateway Publishing®, go to gatewaypublishing.com.

Gateway Press, an imprint of Gateway Publishing
700 Blessed Way
Southlake, TX 76092
gatewaypublishing.com

Printed in the United States of America

21 22 23 24—5 4 3 2 1

Table of contents

How to use this Playbook

BEFORE A NEW season starts in most sports, the coaching staff issues all the players a new playbook. This book contains all the offensive and defensive plays the team will execute in the upcoming season. For the new players (or "rookies"), they will be seeing the team's plays for the first time. For the veteran athletes, the playbook will look familiar, but the coaching staff will have added new plays, adjusted old plays, and removed unsuccessful plays. This book is just such a playbook. You may have received this book from your "coach," in other words, your mentor or oversight. He or she is giving you some important information so you can be a successful ministry "athlete." You might have gotten the book for yourself. Or you may have received the book because you're are part of an accountability group. This playbook doesn't mean you had to be a great athlete in school, but the apostle Paul often compared our work as Christians to the athletic life (see Galatians 2:2, 5:7; Philippians 2:16; 2 Timothy 4:7; and Hebrews 12:1). You are a spiritual athlete, and God wants you to be good at it!

How do athletes usually use playbooks? Once the coaching staff distributes the books, each team member is expected to study them. They are expected to spend many hours going over each play, memorizing them, and knowing their assignments in every one of them. I urge you to spend enough time in this playbook to understand the concepts, explore your own thoughts and feelings, and talk to God about what you are learning.

WHAT IS IN THIS PLAYBOOK?

The *Tested and Approved Mentor's Playbook* is designed for you to use in conjunction with *Tested and Approved: 21 Lessons for Life and Ministry*. I urge you to read each lesson in both books, because doing so will give you a fuller picture of each of the concepts you will be exploring. I want you to think of these two books as spiritual experiences far more than I want you to look at them as mere reading assignments. If you will use them as an opportunity to hear God and respond to Him, you will have a life-changing experience.

This mentor playbook has three major elements, and I believe all of the following are necessary for you to have the fullest experience:

1. LESSON SUMMARY

Every lesson in this book contains a summary of the lesson you will find in *Tested and Approved: 21 Lessons for Life and Ministry*. However, let me remind you that not all of the material is identical; it is complementary. You will expand your own insights if you will read the corresponding lessons in each book. Even so, if you only have access to this book, you will still receive valuable information that will help you as you serve God and minister to others. So, if you only have this book, then use this book. If you have *Tested and Approved: 21 Lessons for Life and Ministry* to use along with this playbook, then all the better.

2. GUIDED SELF-REFLECTION

Each lesson includes a series of questions for reflection. As you consider each question, space is given for you to respond. Answer the questions honestly and prayerfully. Sometimes you will have to dig deep and listen for the Holy Spirit to speak to you as you answer each question. Don't get stuck; if you need to skip a question and come back to it later, then do so. Nevertheless, don't skip questions indefinitely. These questions were designed for you to get to the heart matters of each lesson, and you will get the greatest benefit if you answer all of them.

3. FOCUSED PRAYER PROMPTS

The final section of each lesson is an opportunity for you to talk to God and listen for His responses. These prompts are there to lead you into an honest conversation with God. Space is provided after each prompt for you to expand on your own prayer and, as you listen to the Holy Spirit, you should write what He is saying to you as you pray. *Please don't skip over this section.* I have done my best to share wisdom I have learned from experience and through my relationship with the Lord; however, the Holy Spirit is your best Teacher. You need to hear from Him, or you will miss the most important part of this experience.

THREE SETTINGS

This mentor playbook contains content useful for three different settings.

1. Personal use
2. One-on-one mentoring and oversight
3. Accountability/mentorship group

Each setting comes with unique advantages, experiences, and dynamics. If you use the playbook personally and privately, then you can go at your own pace. You may also feel at liberty to record intimate details that you would otherwise be hesitant to write if you were in a group or in a one-on-one mentoring relationship. Even so, I encourage you to participate with other people if you are able. A group or a mentor will expose you to other viewpoints, help you explore deeper issues, and give you an opportunity to pray in unity with other believers. I would not want to discourage you from using this book privately if that is your only option, but I really believe you will gain more from this experience if you involve others.

One-on-one mentoring is a great way to explore this playbook. Your mentor may either be your oversight in a formal, professional sense, or they may simply be a mature believer you love and trust. In a one-on-one setting, you can share intimate details and spiritual struggles that you may not want to address in a larger group. In this personal setting, your relationship with your mentor will grow, even as you talk and pray through some important and sometimes difficult issues.

You may opt to join a small mentoring group. I'm sure you are aware of the many advantages of small group experiences. A mentoring group has additional benefits. People in your group will be at a compatible place in life and ministry. You will gain knowledge from each other and establish friendships that may last a lifetime.

It is also possible for you to use your playbook in all three settings simultaneously. For example, you could study personally, meet with a mentor or oversight privately, and then participate in a small accountability group. I encourage you to do all you can to pursue an intimate relationship with your Father, to talk to and hear Him.

TIPS FOR USE IN EACH SETTING

As I said previously, this mentor playbook can be used in three settings. In each setting, I will offer some suggestions to ensure a meaningful and successful experience. If you are using this playbook personally and privately, then I will give you tips to give you the best experience for individual use. For mentors and accountability groups, my comments are geared toward *the person who will lead* those sessions. If you are not leading, but you are participating, you will still find helpful ideas in the information that follows.

Tips for players (individual use)

You may realize that the only way for you to explore these lessons is through personal study. If that is the situation, I will give you some helpful tips to get the most of that experience.

1. BEGIN WITH THE RIGHT ATTITUDE

If you are using this book individually and privately, then I want you to consider that you will have an *audience of one—* the Holy Spirit. He is present and available to lead you into all truth (John 16:13). Before you even begin reading each lesson, pause for a moment to quiet your mind, recognize the Holy Spirit's presence, and commit yourself to submit to His voice. Don't think of your experience with these lessons as one more opportunity to gain information. Your attitude makes all the difference. As you read *Tested and Approved: 21 Lessons for Life and Ministry* and this mentor playbook, focus on the Holy Spirit "reading" you.

Search me, O God, and know my heart!
  Try me and know my thoughts! (Psalm 139:23).

2. READ AND MAKE NOTES

Read the lesson in both *Tested and Approved: 21 Lessons for Life and Ministry* and this mentor playbook. As you are reading, make notes about things you want to remember or when the Holy Spirit speaks to your heart and mind about one of the issues you are studying. You may want to make these notes in your personal journal, or you may want to use a notebook specifically dedicated to this experience.

3. ENGAGE IN GUIDED SELF-REFLECTION

Take time to read and answer the questions in the Guided Self-Reflection section. Many of these questions are "heart checks," so don't rush through them. It may take you more than one session to answer all of them because they require a lot of prayerful thought.

4. PRAY WITH A FOCUS

The Focused Prayer Prompts at the end of each lesson are not there to limit your prayers; they were written so your prayers can be focused on the most important issues in each lesson. Again, I would urge you not to rush through them. As you pray through each point, you may wish to expand on it and say even more to the Lord. Above all, listen for the Holy Spirit's voice. What is He saying to you in this lesson?

Tips for team captains
(accountability group leaders)

1. GET READY TO MEET

- Ask God to prepare the hearts and minds of the people in your group. Ask Him to show you how to encourage each person to integrate the principles all of you discover into your daily lives through group discussion and writing in the mentor playbooks.
- Read the lesson in *Tested and Approved: 21 Lessons for Life and Ministry.*
- Read and familiarize yourself with the corresponding lesson in this mentor playbook.
- Plan how much time you'll give to the three sections of the playbook in your meeting (see the suggested schedule below). In case you're unable to get through all of the activities in the time you have allotted, summarize the lesson quickly and encourage participants to read it carefully on their own time (they should have already read it before attending the group meeting), spend the bulk of your time facilitating a discussion on the Guided Personal Reflection section, and then lead the participants through a prayer at the end. Encourage them to spend additional time praying with a partner or alone through the Focused Prayer Prompts.

2. FOLLOW A SCHEDULE

The following is a suggested schedule. You can adjust it according to the needs of the group and how much time you have allotted.

- **Engage** and **Recap** the previous lesson (10 minutes). In the first session you can use this time to introduce the curriculum, the purpose for the group, and for the participants to introduce themselves.

- **Summarize** the lesson (10 minutes).
- **Discuss** the Guided Personal Reflection (30 minutes).
- **Pray** using the Focused Prayer Prompts (15 minutes).

3. HOW TO USE THE CURRICULUM FOR A GROUP

- *Engage*

  Ask the icebreaker question to help get participants talking and feeling comfortable with one another.

- *Recap*

  At the first meeting, provide an overview of *Tested and Approved: 21 Lessons for Life and Ministry* and *Tested and Approved: Mentor Playbook* and encourage everyone to read and prepare before each meeting. For the following meetings, recap the previous lesson and invite members to talk about any new insights they have gained since the last meeting.

- *Summarize*

  Summarize the lesson you are about to discuss.

- *Talk*

  The questions in the Guided Self-Reflection are intentionally open-ended. Use them to help the group members reflect on the lesson's concepts and truths. If you have time, you can pause for the participants to write in their books. If you do not have enough time, discourage participants from writing until after the lesson so they can give their full attention while others are speaking.

- *Pray*

  The Focused Prayer Prompts are designed to lead the participants through the major spiritual issues addressed in each lesson. Ask members to share any of their concerns and then pray together. Be sensitive to the Holy Spirit and the needs of the group. Encourage the participants to pray through the prompts by themselves in private. Tell them to write down additional concerns they have after each prayer prompt. Also, instruct them to listen to the Holy Spirit and record anything He is saying to them.

- *Explore*
  Encourage members to read the next lesson in their mentor playbook and in *Tested and Approved: 21 Lessons for Life and Ministry* before your next meeting. In addition, tell them to complete the written portion in their playbooks from this lesson.

4. OTHER IMPORTANT TIPS FOR THE GROUP LEADER

- Instruct the participants on the importance of confidentiality for this type of group.
- Generate participation and discussion.
- Resist the urge to teach. The goal is for great conversation that leads to discovery.
- Ask open-ended questions—questions that can't be answered with "yes" or "no" (e.g., "What do you think about that?" rather than "Do you agree?")
- When a question arises, ask the group for their input first, instead of immediately answering it yourself.
- Be comfortable with silence. If you ask a question and no one responds, rephrase the question and wait for a response. Your primary role is to create an environment where people feel comfortable to be authentic and participate, not to provide the answers to all of their questions.
- Ask the group members to pray for each other from session to session, especially about key issues that arise during your group time. This is how you begin to build authentic community and encourage spiritual growth within the group.

Tips for coaches
(mentors and oversights)

Relationships are the foundation of ministry. If you want to have the best team, you want to do ministry together for the long haul, so you must care for those relationships. Your relationships are more important that other issues you may face, because relationships endure even when other matters are resolved and long forgotten.

I encourage you to think of the role of the mentor or oversight as similar to that of a parent. What do these roles have in common?

- They are both stewards of life.
- They are serving as God's representatives.
- They both lead people to embrace God's plans and purposes for their lives.
- They are marked by servant leadership rather than control, domination, or manipulation.

Parents are not the same as other family members, such as siblings. Siblings encourage and support each other, while parents guide and invest in their children. Siblings fight alongside each other, while parents fight on behalf of their children. If you are a parent, you already know the difference.

1. BE EMPOWERING

Your goal as a mentor or oversight should be to empower others.

And he gave the apostles, the prophets, the evangelists, the shepherds and teachers, to equip the saints for the work of ministry, for building up the body of Christ, until we all attain to the unity of the faith and of the knowledge of the Son of God, to mature manhood, to the measure of the stature of the fullness of Christ, so that we may no longer be children, tossed to and fro by the waves and carried about by every wind of doctrine, by human cunning, by craftiness in deceitful schemes (Ephesians 4:11–14).

Empowerment is the attitude and the process of investing in people to produce achievable and measurable results.

If you want to become a person who empowers, then open yourself to opportunities for people to use their gifts in ministry. Stretch them and challenge them even while you mentor them to success. Give them adequate resources and clearly defined roles, responsibilities, and parameters. Then provide the best available training to ensure specific values and DNA permeate every area of the ministry. As a person who oversees and mentors, commit yourself to serve those under your care by protecting, directing, encouraging, expecting accountability, and giving constructive feedback. Empowerment will lead to growth, fulfillment, and maximum achievement.

2. BE RELATIONAL

What is relational oversight and mentoring? By *relational* I mean that your relationship with people under your care should be interactive; it involves dialogue rather than your ongoing monologue. It is caring and sensitive, always with an awareness of situations and circumstances. Relational oversight is engaged. As a believer, you know you will be connected to the people under your care throughout eternity, so commit yourself to that eternal perspective. It is supportive, meaning that you will listen, validate, and confirm, but you will not enable bad behavior. And relational oversight is proactive, which means you will always be concerned with what is needed before you are even asked.

A SPECIAL WORD
TO MENTORS AND OVERSIGHTS

If you are a mentor and not in an oversight relationship with the person you are mentoring, the dynamics are different from an oversight relationship. Someone may have approached you to walk with them through these lessons. If that is so, then humbly give God the glory that His work is being recognized in your life. He has entrusted you with a precious task. If you are an oversight and have formal authority over the person you are leading through these lessons, understand this is also an awesome privilege and responsibility to be God's steward and agent in the life of someone God has called for His purpose. In both of these cases, consider the instructions for individual and group use. In a one-on-one setting you will have opportunities to hear and share very personal spiritual concerns and truths. Don't take this solemn task lightly. You may be the very person God has called to bring someone into the fullness of God's call.

GAME TIME!

Now that you have taken the time to understand how to use this book, the rest is up to you, your mentor or oversight, or your accountability group. Most of all, now is an opportunity for the Holy Spirit to do a good work in you. I want you to survive ministry. I want you to *thrive* in ministry. I wrote this because I love you and know God is going to do amazing things in your life. So if you're ready, let the game begin!

Lesson 1

Ministry and life are not fair.

IF YOU GREW up with siblings, then at some point you tattled to your parents about a brother or sister. You probably gave your parents a report about your sibling's bad behavior and then expected them to punish your brother or sister for a wrongdoing according to your definition of justice. If your parents didn't see your sibling's offense in the same way you did, then you naturally cried foul—*no fair!* You counted on your parents to address injustices, and you also had to trust them to determine which actions or infractions required them to intervene. You wanted your parents to act when you experienced injustices from teachers, coaches, or friends, and you counted on them to rightly determine the injustice and guide you to a resolution. That meant you couldn't take matters into your own hands. You would have to trust their ability to determine and extract justice on your behalf.

The Bible offers many accounts that may seem unfair or unjust upon first reading. For example, why did God accept Abel's offering and not Cain's? Or why did God allow Daniel to be thrown into the lion's den when he had been faithful to God in his service to an unbelieving government? In what way is that fair? Why would God allow Saul to hunt down David in an attempt to kill him multiple times? David was God's appointed leader, even described as a man after God's

1

own heart, and anointed to replace Saul as King of Israel. All David's responses and actions were faithful and right, whereas Saul's were driven by jealousy and insecurity. How is that fair? Why did God allow young Joseph's brothers to throw him into a pit and sell him into slavery? Why was Potiphar's wife allowed to unjustly accuse Joseph of a sexual offense, which led to Potiphar throwing him into prison? What had Joseph done to deserve such treatment?

What common theme do these biblical accounts share? With the exception of Cain, each of these biblical people experienced unearned and unjust treatment, but they did not try to stand on the ground of "fairness," nor did they allow themselves to focus on the concept of "justice," even though their lives were radically impacted. Rather they had to depend on their heavenly Father to determine what was just and right for them regardless of their feelings. Their trust in God's goodness was the right response.

You and I can also follow this pattern. In reality, life isn't fair. As we experience injustice and unfairness, we have the opportunity to allow our faith to arise. Cain also had this opportunity and failed. God asked him why he was angry and why his countenance had fallen. Then God asked this important question: "If you do well, will you not be accepted?" Is this not also a question to us? The Lord is asking us, "If you will trust Me and make your response based on that trust, do you have faith that everything will be fine? Do you not know everything will work out for your good?" Cain wouldn't listen to or trust in the Lord, so he took matters into his own murderous hands.

GUIDED SELF-EXAMINATION

1. What pattern do you follow as you respond to unfair situations in your life?

_____

_____

_____

_____

_____

_____

_____

2. Is there a current unfair situation you are upset about? Look back over the last few years of your life and take an "inventory of the unfairness" you have experienced. Dig deep and be honest.

- In what ways have you been treated unfairly by family?

_____

_____

_____

_____

_____

_____

_____

_____

- In what ways were you treated unfairly in school by a fellow student, teacher, or coach?

_____

_____

_____

_____

_____

_____

_____

- How have you responded when you have been treated unjustly by society?

_____

_____

_____

_____

_____

_____

_____

_____

- How have you been treated unfairly in your professional life? Perhaps you have been overlooked for a promotion, used or abused by a boss, or mistreated by coworkers.

_____

_____

_____

_____

_____

_____

_____

- In the unfair situations you have experienced, how have you responded to God? Have you blamed Him for not acting to protect you from unfairness and injustice? Have you experienced depression? Have you responded in faith?

_____

_____

_____

_____

_____

_____

_____

_____

Like Cain, you also have a decision to make. You can allow your "face to fall" and take matters into you own hands, attempting to bring an end to the person or situation you blame for your injustice. Or you can open your heart to the Lord. You can compare yourself with someone else and conclude that what you have experienced is unfair as you seethe with anger over the injustice. Or you can take your pain to the Lord. Maybe you have done things for which you are ashamed because you felt you were treated unfairly. Spend some time with the Lord and be honest with Him. You may also wish to pray with your mentor or accountability group. Yes, God's statement to Cain is true for each of us in these situations: Sin is right behind the door, but grace is on your side of the door. If you look to God and trust Him with this injustice, then He will work His good purposes on your behalf.

FOCUSED PRAYER PROMPTS

Here are some prayer prompts to help you as you apply this lesson to your life:

- Lord, I have been treated unfairly in these areas of my life:

_____

_____

_____

Ministry and life are not fair.

_____

_____

_____

_____

_____

- I have taken matters into my own hands responding in these sinful ways because I was hurt and angry:

_____

_____

_____

_____

_____

_____

_____

_____

- I ask you to forgive me for these actions of mistrust toward you:

_____

_____

_____

_____

_____

_____

_____

_____

- I renounce sin, including the sin of comparison, and turn away from it. I will do these things to make right any wrongs I have done:

_____

_____

_____

_____

_____

_____

_____

Lesson 2

Ministry is about people before it is about results.

HAVE YOU HEARD that the Bible is really a love story? It is about God's great love for humanity and the extent He went to develop and keep His relationship with each of us. The Bible begins with God creating a garden and placing Adam and Eve in it. There were no weeds or thorns. The plants grew from the dew. The Lord walked in the garden in the cool of the day to fellowship and interact with Adam and Eve.

We don't know exactly how long these walks took place. It could have been days, weeks, months, or even years. Time was not an issue in the garden. The first couple was free to explore the creation and interact with each other. They could also explore and develop their relationship with the living, loving Creator. As they related to Him, God told them they could eat freely of the things in the garden, except for one of the trees in the center of the garden.

The Lord loved Adam and Eve, making every provision for their well-being. However, the first couple didn't do what God told them. Instead they ate of the tree that God told them not to touch. The devil, in the form of a serpent, seduced them with lies and trickery, leading them into willful sin. In their disobedience, everything changed. It separated them from a loving God, breaking a relationship the couple alone could not repair.

This human disobedience irreparably damaged their nature, changing it to one that naturally reproduced sin in their offspring, who then followed with their own independent rebellious acts against God. So then, the Bible's great love story is one of redemption and restoration of that relationship. God orchestrated a grand plan to redeem and restore His relationship with all humanity. He bridged the gap through the righteousness of His own Son, Jesus Christ. The Bible reveals that God loved us so much He gave His Son so that anyone who believed in Him could be restored, both now and forever (John 3:16)!

If you want to comprehend God and serve His interests here on earth, then you must understand His relational nature, because He loves us so much. The big question each of us must answer about our lives is this: *Are we pursuing a personal, intimate relationship with God, or are we working to appease Him and earn His approval?* The reason this question is so important is that it influences not only our relationship with God but also with others. If we try to relate with God primarily based on what we produce, then we will tend to relate with others from that same perspective. We will accept or reject people based on what they can produce rather than on who they are becoming. We will judge them and their actions rather than loving them into a place of unity, agreement, and a surrendered relationship with God. We must be careful not to value people based on the results they produce. Otherwise, when they can't perform according to our expectations, we will then be tempted to discard them and move on to someone else who can give us the results we want.

God values people. The way we work with others is a testing ground for God to develop, train, and correct us. Through our own free choice, we can elect to be lazy, self-willed, and independent, which will sideline us from God's purposes for us. By His nature, He is patient, kind, and longsuffering for His children. As God's sons and daughters, we should reflect those same qualities as we relate to others. Our focus should be on molding, shaping, and developing them through our love, care, and commitment.

GUIDED SELF-EXAMINATION

1. How do you relate to people? Do you sometimes interact with them based on what they can do for you or what they can produce? How often do you relate to them based on who God created them to be?

_____

_____

_____

_____

_____

_____

_____

_____

2. Describe how you see your relationship with God.

_____

_____

_____

_____

_____

_____

_____

_____

3. Take an honest inventory of the broken relationships in your life. Think back over the last few years and make a list of people with whom have had broken relationships. Write down the names of those who have been close to you but aren't any more. There may be very good reasons that certain individuals no longer hold the place they once did in your life. However, some people may be on your list because they failed to meet your expectations, so you dropped them.

_____

_____

_____

_____

_____

_____

_____

_____

_____

_____

4. Is there someone you are feeling negative feelings toward and withdrawing from right now? Describe the situation.

_____

_____

_____

_____

_____

_____

_____

5. Can you think of a relationship that you would say serves no good purpose in your life? What is that situation and why?

_____

_____

_____

_____

_____

_____

_____

6. What are some of your close relationships and what do they do for you? Why are they important to you?

- What does your spouse do for you?

_____

_____

_____

_____

_____

- Who are your three closest friends, and what do they do for you?

_____

_____

_____

_____

_____

_____

_____

_____

_____

Ministry is about people before it is about results.

- Who are your closest work associates? What are the reasons you are close to them?

_____

_____

_____

_____

_____

_____

_____

_____

_____

FOCUSED PRAYER PROMPTS

Here are some prayer prompts to help you as you apply this lesson to your life:

- Holy Spirit, bring to my mind those who have hurt me and I know I need to forgive. Help me as I agree with You to forgive them right now.

_____

_____

_____

_____

_____

_____

- Work on my heart so that I can show more appreciation for the people You have put in my life.

_____

_____

_____

_____

_____

- Draw me closer to Yourself. I want to have a deeper intimacy with You.

_____

_____

_____

_____

_____

_____

_____

Lesson 3

We will be known
by the fruit we produce.

BUSINESSES TODAY FOCUS on brand identity and social media positioning. They create social media posts to promote their products and support their identities. Celebrities and politicians spend many hours and much money establishing and protecting their reputations and the brands they represent. Do these public figures and companies know something that we should pay attention to in our own lives? The Bible seems to say so. In Proverbs 22:1, King Solomon wrote,

> A good name is to be chosen rather than great riches,
>   and favor is better than silver or gold.

How much time do you spend thinking about your "name" or your reputation and the fruit your life produces? How much concern do you give to the character and integrity that your life reflects? Have you thought about the values your life reflects and how you are creating a culture and heritage for your family?

In 1 Samuel 15, the prophet Samuel gave King Saul an assignment. He told Saul to attack the Amalekites and completely destroy them and everything they owned. Saul did attack and defeat the Amalekites, but he didn't destroy everyone and everything after his army won. Instead, he spared the Amalekite king and kept some of the livestock and property. Saul didn't consider that his actions would have such dire consequences. As he was celebrating the victory, God was already regretting that He had made Saul king. The Lord sent Samuel to confront Saul about his half-hearted, disobedient actions. Samuel told him that the Lord had selected another king to take Saul's place. Saul immediately regretted his behavior and wanted to change the result, so he pleaded for Samuel to return with him before the people. Saul wanted to invoke Samuel's name and reputation to cover his sin, hoping that the people would see him positively. If Saul had only understood God's desire for obedience over sacrifice and considered the consequences of his actions before it was too late, then he might have done the right thing and remained as king. Samuel's good name would not save Saul, because Saul had squandered his own reputation.

A good name is worth more than great riches. Your name reflects the reputation of your character and the fruit of your actions. Your values form the foundation for your actions and behavior. If you choose to act in ways you know are wrong, then your bad reputation will follow. If you choose to obey God with your actions, then your good reputation will follow as well.

GUIDED SELF-EXAMINATION

1. When was the last time you considered your reputation and the fruit your life reflects? What was the catalyst that led you to consider your reputation? What change did you adopt as you considered your reputation?

_____

_____

We will be known by the fruit we produce.

_____

_____

_____

_____

_____

_____

_____

2. If someone were to write a statement about your reputation, then what would you ultimately like it to say? Would they be able to say that right now? Why or why not?

_____

_____

_____

_____

_____

_____

_____

_____

3. Describe a time when your actions and behavior did not represent the values and fruit that you want your life to reflect.

_____

_____

_____

_____

_____

_____

_____

4. List five core values that you want your life to reflect.

_____

_____

_____

_____

_____

_____

_____

5. Who are some of people who you hold as models for the fruit you would like to see in your own life?

_____

_____

_____

_____

_____

_____

_____

6. Where have you seen "disconnect" in someone else's life, meaning that they were hypocritical and their actions did not match their stated values? How did these actions influence your opinion of their reputation?

_____

_____

_____

_____

_____

_____

_____

FOCUSED PRAYER PROMPTS

Here are some prayer prompts to help you as you apply this lesson to your life:

- Holy Spirit, bring me to a place of freedom and fruitfulness in my life. Show me how I can have the kind of reputation that will bring glory to my Father.

_____

_____

_____

_____

_____

_____

_____

- Help me to build endurance and patience so that You can form me into a person who consistently reflects God's character in my life. Show me the ways I have let impatience rob me of a good reputation.

_____

_____

_____

_____

We will be known by the fruit we produce.

_____

_____

_____

_____

- Show me how to reflect Your values in my life. I will work to transfer those values to my family in the following ways:

_____

_____

_____

_____

_____

_____

_____

_____

Lesson 4

Success is a process.

THE BIBLE GIVES us a great promise in Jeremiah 29:11. There God tells His people that He has plans for us, and His plans are for our good and not for evil, to give us a hope and a future. He has put within each of us an appetite to know and fulfill the purpose He has given us. We are on a journey to find our purpose. This is the destination where we will be able to deploy the gifts God has given us as we serve and operate according to His plan. Your true success will not be measured by the size of your salary, your title, or the accolades and rewards you receive along the way. Success, from God's perspective, comes as you discover His purpose for your life and then act to fulfill.

Along the journey, we will face obstacles to overcome. Our character will be tested, shaped, and developed. And we will grow in faith as we learn to lean on God and His Word more than our own understanding. Yes, there will be times when a road you go down won't make any sense. Sometimes you will question the path because the landscape is unfamiliar and unexpected. Perhaps you will take a turn off of the superhighway that leads to wealth, fame, and status. Your every instinct will tell you to go back to the main road because it will lead to your fulfillment. You may tell God that you want to take over the navigation. You may hear voices both within and without telling you this road won't lead you where you want to go. But stay *the* course!

How can you know you are on the right course? Check the map! God's Word is your navigation tool, so review it and make your decisions according to its directions. It will tell you where you are and which way you should go. Maybe you've made a wrong turn, but you are not on your own. The Word and the Spirit are there to guide you back to the right path. Find other trusted travelers to help you read the map and hear from the Mapmaker. These mentors love God and are committed to your well-being. Trust them.

To use another metaphor: At times you will feel as though you are a pilot flying a plane in stormy weather. You won't be able to fly by normal *visual flight rules*; this is an *instrument only* flight. You must trust your instruments to get you safely to your destination. Your flight plan has been determined by God. The Holy Spirit is your ground control, and He is guiding you on the right flight path. Trust His guidance and lean on your instrument, the Word of God.

Success is a process that involves hearing God's plan, believing that He blesses and rewards those who seek His purposes, and being convinced that He will lead, guide, and instruct as you obey Him. In the process, do not forget that He is in charge. If you don't allow Him to lead, then you are in charge, or even worse, you are being driven along by the influences of this world and the spiritual forces who want to destroy you and lead you away from your God-given destination.

GUIDED SELF-EXAMINATION

1. What journey are you taking? Is it one of personal success and fame? Or are you seeking God's purpose for your life?

Do you know your purpose? Can you describe it in a few sentences?

_____

_____

_____

_____

_____

_____

_____

_____

_____

_____

2. As you think about God's purpose being expressed through your life, what would that look like for you?

_____

_____

_____

_____

_____

_____

_____

_____

3. Have you felt lost in your journey to discover and operate in your purpose? What are some of the feelings you have related to that journey?

_____

_____

_____

_____

_____

_____

_____

_____

_____

4. Have you tried to take any shortcuts to the success you have wanted in your life? What happened and what did you discover in the process? As you read Proverbs 12:27, how has your experience been similar or different?

_____

_____

Success is a process.

_____

_____

_____

_____

_____

_____

_____

_____

_____

FOCUSED PRAYER PROMPTS

Here are some prayer prompts to help you as you apply this lesson to your life:

- Lord, I ask You to reveal and clarify to me the purpose You have for my life. I am listening for Your voice.

_____

_____

_____

_____

_____

_____

_____

_____

- Give me diligence to remain faithful along the journey.

_____

_____

_____

_____

_____

_____

- Lord, restore focus when I get off track and clarity when I become confused.

_____

_____

_____

_____

_____

_____

Success is a process.

_____

_____

- Renew my faith in Your purpose for my life and forgive me
  for times I have doubted Your guidance.

_____

_____

_____

_____

_____

_____

_____

Lesson 5

Accountability is a good thing.

SOME PEOPLE DISCOUNT the importance of accountability, opting for total freedom to do what they want. They move forward only if they feel it is best for them, regardless of the ways it affects others. Still others make the claim that they are accountable, yet upon closer scrutiny, they have never been tested by disagreement or conflict. We show accountability through surrender and submission, humbly allowing our hearts to be corrected, even when we disagree. Ultimately, our accountability to human authorities really shows that we trust in God and His sovereign control in our lives.

Asa was a good king who ruled in Judah, according to 2 Chronicles 14. He did what was good and right in the sight of the Lord. Then just two chapters later, Asa sinned against the Lord by taking actions he thought were best to solve a problem rather than submitting it to God or prophetic leadership. By doing this, he missed an opportunity to defeat King Baasha, an evil king who ruled Israel when the nation was divided. King Baasha constantly attacked Asa's territory and remained a thorn in his side. During one of those attacks, Asa took independent action. Baasha came against him with his army and mounted a siege against Jerusalem. Baasha would not allow people, goods, or supplies to go in or out of the city. He intended to bring the people of Jerusalem to their knees through the threat of starvation and the strangling of the supply line.

As things grew more desperate, Asa failed to look to God for deliverance; rather he took matters into his own hands, setting an alliance with Ben-Hadad, the king of Syria. The prophet Hanani confronted Asa over his missed opportunity to consult the Lord. Then Hanani told him that because he did not look to God, King Baasha would not suffer defeat or surrender from that time on. Asa would have ongoing wars with King Baasha. All this happened because Asa would not turn to God, but instead he sought help from a man, King Ben-Hadad.

How can such a tragedy happen to a good king? It comes through independence, pride, and a lack of accountability. Ultimately, although he was a good king, he was not accountable to anyone, especially God. If we are not careful, then we will follow the same path as Asa when we face threatening circumstances. We need accountability and the protection it provides.

GUIDED SELF-EXAMINATION

To whom are you accountable? Think of this question another way: *Who can correct me?* You may have multiple people who can do this in your life, or you may have no one to whom you are accountable. If you can't honestly name anyone to whom you are accountable, then you are in a dangerous place that may seriously impact your life.

A wise man is full of strength,
    and a man of knowledge enhances his might,
for by wise guidance you can wage your war,
    and in abundance of counselors there is victory.

Wisdom is too high for a fool;
    in the gate he does not open his mouth (Proverbs 24:5–7).

1. To whom in your life are you accountable? Make a list of the people. How does each person hold you accountable?

_____

_____

_____

_____

_____

_____

_____

_____

_____

2. Describe a time when you found accountability to be a struggle through disagreement and submission over an issue where there was disagreement.

_____

_____

_____

_____

_____

_____

_____

_____

_____

3. What emotions did you experience as you finally surrendered to accountability? If you did not surrender, what were the consequences?

_____

_____

_____

_____

_____

_____

_____

_____

4. Has God ever asked you to be accountable to someone who doesn't share your values or to someone you don't respect? If so, describe that situation and how you arrived at a place of submission.

_____

_____

Accountability is a good thing.

_____

_____

_____

_____

_____

_____

_____

_____

5. Can you recall situations when you resisted authority, even refusing to submit to someone to whom you were supposed to be accountable? If so, list some of those situations and describe what happened.

_____

_____

_____

_____

_____

_____

_____

_____

_____

_____

_____

_____

FOCUSED PRAYER PROMPTS

Here are some prayer prompts to help you as you apply this lesson to your life:

- Holy Spirit, reveal to me how You view accountability.

_____

_____

_____

_____

_____

_____

_____

- Lord, I confess to You my pride, independence, and any other attitudes that have reflected my independence. Forgive me and change my heart to accept Your authority and accountability to those You have put in that position in my life.

_____

_____

Accountability is a good thing.

_____

_____

_____

_____

_____

_____

- I ask You to lead me into relationships with people who love
  me and You and to whom I can willingly submit to accountability.

_____

_____

_____

_____

_____

_____

_____

Lesson 6

Every generation
is responsible
to build wealth.

HAVE YOU EVER considered yourself both a *wealth builder* and a *consumer*? It is true, you are a mixture of both. Now ask yourself which one of those qualities most accurately describes your attitudes, actions, and lifestyle? What are you doing with the resources you have been given? Are you using them to grow more resources, even while you are enjoying their fruit and blessing your family and others? Or, are you consuming them for your own needs and pleasures with little consideration of others or of the legacy you might leave behind for the generations who follow? Do you manage your life's resources considering God's purpose in entrusting them to you?

Exodus 20:5–6 gives us one of the Bible's greatest revelations and promises. Those verses contain a foundational truth on which I have built my life, family, and career for forty-plus years: "I the LORD your God am a jealous God, visiting the iniquity of the fathers *on the children to the third and the fourth generation of those who hate me,* but showing steadfast love to *thousands [of generations]* of those who love me and keep my commandments" (Exodus 20:5–6, emphasis added).

An iniquity is a "bent" or "leaning" toward a behavior, which then gets passed to subsequent generations. Iniquities might include alcoholism, drug addiction, poverty, mental illness, or any other harmful characteristic that has multigenerational connections in our families. God says those harmful characteristics will influence three and four generations unless He is involved in our lives. However, out of His loving heart God offers each of us a lasting promise that if we will love and serve Him, then He will show His steadfast love to us through a thousand generations!

This promise encourages me because it is personal to me and it is generational to my children and grandchildren and beyond. It says that the actions and decisions of my life will have multigenerational influence and impact. If previous generations in my family have been wealth building, I can carry on their work in my generation and pass it along to the generations that follow me. If previous generations in my family have been consumers controlled by their iniquities, I can break those iniquities by turning my heart to God and become the first wealth-builder generation in my family. God says I can make a decision in my life that will have life-changing effect in its multigenerational impact upon my family and the heritage that follows in future generations.

In Matthew 25, Jesus told a parable about three servants whose master entrusted them with talents (worth a significant sum of money) based on their abilities. Each of the servants was told to steward their talents for the master while he was away on a trip. Two of the servants were builders who took their talents and invested them. These two servants doubled what had been entrusted to them. The third servant was a consumer who buried his talent because he was too fearful to risk the possibility of losing his master's resources. A fearful mindset is even worse than a consuming mindset alone, because it wastes the resources given to us on our own pleasures without considering God's purpose or the needs of generations to come. This servant's lack of effort meant that he buried the resources given to him. This mindset is certainly a close cousin to the consumer mindset with its selfish entitlement and waste of resources with little thought of the next generation or the heritage it is leaving behind.

What is the emphasis of your life? How are you using the resources God has entrusted to you? As you think about these questions, also consider how God defines wealth. You will probably need to broaden your definition to include more than just money and material resources. God's understanding of wealth is much broader. It includes your relationships, the knowledge you gain from education or life experience, your financial assets, your reputation and influence, and the spiritual blessings that come from knowing and serving God.

GUIDED SELF-EXAMINATION

1. Which describes you more accurately, *consumer* or *wealth builder*? What did you choose and why?

_____

_____

_____

_____

_____

_____

_____

2. Are you aware of family iniquities in your great-grandparents, grandparents, parents, or siblings? List them.

_____

_____

_____

_____

_____

_____

_____

3. What are God's blessings you recognize in your life? List them.

_____

_____

_____

_____

_____

_____

_____

4. What are the ways you and members of your family have enjoyed God's goodness while building wealth for the next generation? List them.

_____

_____

_____

_____

_____

_____

_____

5. List the different types of wealth that have been entrusted to you:

- In relationships

_____

_____

_____

_____

_____

_____

- In knowledge and education

- In financial resources

- In family reputation and influence

- In life experience along with wisdom

_____

_____

_____

_____

_____

- In spiritual blessings and heritage

_____

_____

_____

_____

FOCUSED PRAYER PROMPTS

Here are some prayer prompts to help you as you apply this lesson to your life:

- Lord Jesus, I ask You to break family iniquities in my life and to replace them with Your gifts and blessings.

_____

_____

_____

- Father, give me wisdom and faith as I take the resources You have entrusted to me so I can build wealth to pass on to the next generation.

- Holy Spirit, show me any area in my life that reflects a consuming rather than a wealth-building mindset.

Every generation is responsible to build wealth.

_____

_____

_____

_____

_____

- Lord, for all You have given me, I thank you. Today, I declare that I want to be a good steward with all You have given me. I want to be a wealth builder here on earth in a way that will also lay up treasures in heaven.

_____

_____

_____

_____

_____

_____

_____

Lesson 7

Take responsibility
for your mistakes.

WHY IS IT so hard to admit when we are wrong? Why do we become so defensive? Why do we become stubborn when we are confronted with our failed efforts, especially when we are the major contributors to those failures? Why is our default to blame others for the outcome? Why is it our habit to make excuses rather than taking ownership of our mistakes? The answers to these questions provide the keys to unlocking our ability to take responsibility for our mistakes.

In Genesis 3 God has an encounter with Adam and Eve. Previously, God told the human couple they could enjoy all the fruit of the Garden of Eden, but they were not to eat from one of the trees in the garden's center. Satan, in the form of a serpent, lied, tempted, and enticed them to eat from precisely *that* tree! Then the couple yielded to the temptation and ate from the forbidden tree. After their act of disobedience, God entered the garden and called to them but they hid themselves. When they finally stepped forward to face God, they told Him they were embarrassed because they were naked.

[The man] said, "I heard the sound of you in the garden, and I was afraid, because I was naked, and I hid myself." He said,

"Who told you that you were naked? Have you eaten of the tree of which I commanded you not to eat?" The man said, "The woman whom you gave to be with me, she gave me fruit of the tree, and I ate." Then the LORD God said to the woman, "What is this that you have done?" The woman said, "The serpent deceived me, and I ate" (Genesis 3:10–13).

Adam and Eve could not or would not admit they had done wrong; rather they became defensive and pointed fingers of blame at each other and God. Their sinful act became ingrained in human nature, and all humanity must now overcome it. This is a nature bent on defending our actions, excusing our failed efforts, and blaming others for the negative results.

GUIDED SELF-EXAMINATION

1. Have you been blaming someone else for problems in your life, such as your parents, boss, spouse, or other circumstances you feel were set against your success? Take an honest inventory of who you have been blaming.

_____

_____

_____

_____

_____

_____

_____

2. What are the top five problems you are dealing with right now?

_____

_____

_____

_____

_____

_____

_____

_____

3. As you consider those problems, how have you contributed to them?

_____

_____

_____

_____

_____

_____

_____

_____

4. List one or more situations in which you did not achieve the results you expected.

_____

_____

_____

_____

_____

_____

_____

5. What are the reasons why the expected results were not produced?

_____

_____

_____

_____

_____

_____

_____

6. Knowing what you know now, what would you do differently to get different results?

_____

_____

_____

_____

_____

_____

_____

FOCUSED PRAYER PROMPTS

Here are some prayer prompts to help you as you apply this lesson to your life:

- Lord, I want to forgive myself for failing to meet my own and Your expectations. Reveal to me how I can extend grace to myself.

_____

_____

_____

_____

_____

_____

_____

_____

- Help me to forgive those who were part of the problem that led to the failure.

_____

_____

_____

_____

_____

_____

- Father, free me from anger and defensiveness over these issues.

_____

_____

_____

_____

_____

_____

Take responsibility for your mistakes.

_____

_____

- I want Your purposes to be fully developed in my life, and I
  ask You to be my guide.

_____

_____

_____

_____

_____

_____

_____

Lesson 8

Respect and honor the past.

WHEN JESUS' DISCIPLES came to Him with a request for Him to teach them how to pray, He gave them what is commonly called "The Lord's Prayer" (Matthew 6:5–15; Luke 11:1–13). Jesus opens the prayer with a very important statement: "Our Father in heaven, *hallowed* be your name" (Matthew 6:9, emphasis added). *Hallowed* is not a commonly used word today, but it means "sacred, set apart, made holy, greatly revered, or honored." "Hallow," used as a verb, means to "calculate, estimate, or prepare to create something."

Each generation must begin its journey by coming to terms with the previous work of their fathers' and mothers' generations, by making space for the past while going into the future. As believers, we hallow a space for God's work, even while we make room to incorporate what we have learned from the past. We then bring what we have learned into new expressions for our generation. We cannot begin with a blank slate *(tabula rasa)*, nor can we accomplish dynamic progress across generations by ignoring or destroying the work of those who have gone before. Beware of blaming, belittling, insulting, disparaging, or rejecting their influence and instruction before you give it thoughtful consideration. God wants us to build new and greater expressions of His work, but we need the influence of our spiritual fathers and mothers.

King Rehoboam was Solomon's son who ascended to the throne of Israel following his father's death. As Rehoboam sought to solidify his power, he sent for his father's advisors. The citizens had asked Rehoboam to lighten the load Solomon put on them. These advisors who had served Solomon were older and more experienced, so they drew from their historical perspective. "And they said to him, 'If you will be a servant to this people today and serve them, and speak good words to them when you answer them, then they will be your servants forever'" (1 Kings 12:7).

Rehoboam, thinking himself already wise, ignored the older advisors' counsel and took the advice of his young friends who had grown up with him. They recommended for him to respond with firm authority to solidify the kingdom under his rule, and they suggested he tell the people, "My little finger is thicker than my father's thighs. And now, whereas my father laid on you a heavy yoke, I will add to your yoke. My father disciplined you with whips, but I will discipline you with scorpions" (1 Kings 12:10–11). Rehoboam refused to honor the past or to make room for the counsel his father's advisors, and he rejected their advice to make his own way. His choice led to disaster and the end of the united kingdom of Israel.

The focus of this lesson is to look at how we can respect and honor the past, all the while making a space for God's work in our lives. How can we respect and give honor to our fathers and mothers by making space to apply their wisdom, training, and experience? For us to do this, we must contextualize the instruction and influence we received, and then make relevant application in the current generation. This effort takes thoughtful work and respectful digging so we can understand and apply the lessons and advice from the past to our present circumstances.

GUIDED SELF-EXAMINATION

1. What is/was your relationship with your fathers and mothers: meaning your father/mother, grandfather/grandmother, and great grandfather/grandmother? Were they present in your life? What did they teach you that you can apply to your life today?

_____

_____

_____

_____

_____

_____

_____

_____

2. Do you hear your fathers' and mothers' voices as you address circumstances you face today? If so, are they voices of encouragement? Are they beneficial voices that give instruction that you can draw from in a current situation? Do you generally honor or dishonor the influence and instruction you received from them?

_____

_____

_____

_____

_____

_____

_____

_____

_____

3. List five things your father or mother taught you. Are any of these instructions ones that you outright reject as irrelevant to you and your generation? Why or why not?

_____

_____

_____

_____

_____

_____

_____

_____

_____

_____

_____

_____

4. Discuss your relationship with your father or mother and
what impact it has had on the way you relate to God.

_____

_____

_____

_____

_____

_____

_____

_____

_____

_____

5. List one or more situations where you disregarded your
father's or mother's advice or teaching.

_____

_____

_____

_____

_____

_____

_____

_____

_____

_____

6. What has happened because of you ignoring that advice.?

_____

_____

_____

_____

_____

_____

_____

_____

_____

_____

7. If you are a parent, how will you teach/influence your child differently from the way your mother or father did with you?

_____

_____

_____

_____

_____

_____

_____

_____

8. Not all parents act responsibly toward their children. That may be your experience. If so, how are you processing your past experiences? How are you dealing with issues such as unforgiveness, shame, and anger? Did someone else serve in the role of a parent in your life, and what lessons did you learn from that person?

_____

_____

_____

_____

_____

_____

_____

_____

_____

_____

_____

PRAYER PROMPTS

Here are some prayer prompts to help you as you apply this lesson to your life:

- Father, forgive me for any of the sinful ways I have responded to the failings of my father and mother.

_____

_____

_____

_____

_____

_____

_____

- Lord Jesus, I ask You to heal any hurts that have turned into barriers that prevent me from applying lessons from my father or mother. Help me to honor the past as I do it for Your glory.

_____

_____

_____

_____

_____

_____

_____

- Lord, lead me as I try to establish a heritage for future genera-tions in my family, work, and ministry.

_____

_____

_____

_____

_____

_____

_____

Lesson 9

Excellence is a reflection of effort and attitude.

WHEN YOU THINK of *excellence,* what comes to your mind? Do you think of *expensive*? Maybe you think of the *best* of something. Or you might think of *having no rivals.* Would you say that LeBron James is excellent at basketball? Or is Bill Gates excellent at business? Are you an excellent student, parent, employee, athlete? The list could go on.

King David's son Solomon was excellent in all his ways. His reputation for excellence spread everywhere. He became so famous for his excellence that the Queen of Sheba traveled a long distance to witness it firsthand. In 1 Kings 10:4–5, she gave this assessment: "When the queen of Sheba had seen all the wisdom of Solomon, the house that he had built, the food of his table, the seating of his officials, and the attendance of his servants, their clothing, his cupbearers, and his burnt offerings that he offered at the house of the LORD, *there was no more breath in her*" (emphasis added).

Was the queen impressed by Solomon's great wealth? His wealth certainly was great, but what really amazed her was the way he conducted himself and his kingdom. Solomon's efforts bore the fruit of excellence. Excellence is not about money; it is about the wisdom reflected in the way we go about our business. It displays discernment, which is then reflected in our attitudes and efforts. Simply stated, excellence is doing the best with what we have available to us in every situation; making the most of the talents and resources God has given us.

Long before the Queen of Sheba arrived on the scene, God visited with Solomon as he followed his father David and stepped into his role as king. In 1 Kings 3:5, "the LORD appeared to Solomon in a dream by night, and God said, 'Ask what I shall give you.'" Now, can you imagine God coming to you with a blank check and giving you that opportunity? But what did Solomon do? He didn't ask for wealth or victory over his enemies. Instead, Solomon asked for "an understanding mind to govern your people, that I may discern between good and evil" (1 Kings 3:9). As a result, Solomon's reign was marked by the excellence that the Queen of Sheba heard about and then witnessed with her own eyes.

Excellence compares to influence much like wattage relates to the brightness of a lightbulb. If you want to have a brighter bulb, then you'll need more wattage. And if you want to have greater influence, then be excellent in all your efforts. God is calling you to excellence, and He will simply not allow you to move on, nor will He grant you a greater platform of influence, if you neglect excellence. God has given you the responsibility to steward the talents, abilities, and resources He entrusted to you. He expects you to use them to display and produce excellence for His glory.

GUIDED SELF-EXAMINATION

What are you doing with the resources God has given to you? Do you do your best with every opportunity? Or do you gauge your effort depending on who is involved or how much benefit you will receive?

1. List five recent opportunities you have been given, and then rate the results as excellent, good, poor, or failing. Why did you rate each of them the way you did?

_____

_____

_____

_____

_____

_____

_____

_____

_____

_____

_____

2. Supply and describe an example of an opportunity you would rate as poor or failing because you expected perfect results.

_____

_____

_____

_____

_____

_____

_____

_____

_____

3. Now rate yourself in relation to this opportunity on a scale of 1 to 10 (with 1 being lowest) in these ways:

- Effort given to preparation   _____ rating
- Engagement in the moment   _____ rating
- Effective use of the available resources   _____ rating
- Actual results compared to projected results _____ rating
- Average of the four previous answers   _____ rating

4. If perfection is not the standard of excellence, then what would you say it is? Define excellence in your own words, then briefly discuss your definition in the lines below.

_____

_____

_____

_____

_____

_____

Excellence is a reflection of effort and attitude.

_____

_____

_____

_____

FOCUSED PRAYER PROMPTS

Here are some prayer prompts to help you as you apply this lesson to your life:

- Dear Father, I want to be diligent in all my efforts. Grow the desire for excellence in me. Change my heart and mind to reflect Your desires.

_____

_____

_____

_____

_____

_____

- Lord, I am facing opportunities that give me concern. I always want to be excellent. Help me in each of these situations.

_____

_____

_____

_____

_____

_____

_____

- Father, I think of times when I was not excellent. I know the devil is an accuser. Help me to hear Your voice and to ignore his. Remove any guilt or condemnation that I have allowed to enter my mind and heart. Replace them with faith so that I can give my very best to every opportunity.

_____

_____

_____

_____

_____

_____

- Thank You, God, for increasing the "wattage" of my influence as You devote my efforts and attitudes toward excellence.

_____

_____

Excellence is a reflection of effort and attitude.

_____

_____

_____

_____

_____

_____

Lesson 10

Live your life in a godly rhythm.

How would describe your current stress? Have you set aside a day for rest each week? Are you the kind of person who takes your responsibilities seriously? Would you say you have a need to control people or situations? How good are you at delegating tasks to others? If you delegate, does it cause you anxiety? Do you find yourself looking over the shoulder of the person to whom you assigned the task, or do you micromanage their work?

When you read the above questions, how do you think they relate to the concept of "rhythm"? The answer is *everything*. You see, busy people get things done, and then they are given more to do. If you want to grow an organization, see it thrive, and expand your personal interests, it will require that you learn to structure and prioritize your life in a godly rhythm.

Here is a simple truth about rhythm: there will always be more on your plate than you have time to do. You can always muffle the nagging feeling in your heart or even ignore your loved ones' concerns for you. You know when your life is out of rhythm. You can keep saying, "Just one more thing, one more season, and then everything will return to normal." Stop fooling yourself. As parents, we know when it's bedtime that our children will always find "one more thing" to do. But as a parent, you also know that tomorrow will come regardless of how late you stay up the night before. The same is true for us. Even if you *finally* finish this season, a new one is coming with new demands and new responsibilities. If you don't learn how to operate in this season, what makes you think tomorrow's will be any better?

The Lord handpicked Moses to lead the children of Israel out of Egyptian bondage and into the Promised Land. The Lord charged him to lead a "stiff-necked" (Exodus 32:9) and "rebellious" (Deuteronomy 9:7) people. Moses had a very difficult job with daily pressures and unrealistic expectations from the people. He took on the responsibility to resolve disputes and was often met with resistance both to him and to God. As the Hebrew people were on their journey, Moses' father-in-law Jethro approached him.

> The next day Moses sat to judge the people, and the people stood around Moses from morning till evening. When Moses' father-in-law saw all that he was doing for the people, he said, "What is this that you are doing for the people? Why do you sit alone, and all the people stand around you from morning till evening?" And Moses said to his father-in-law, "Because the people come to me to inquire of God" (Exodus 18:13–15).

Jethro offered sage advice to help Moses resolve his rhythm problem. He told Moses to "look for able men from all the people, men who fear God, who are trustworthy and hate a bribe, and place such men over the people as chiefs of thousands, of hundreds, of fifties, and of tens" (Exodus 18:21). When Moses followed Jethro's advice, his life soon returned to a godly rhythm.

This passage of Scripture identifies another kind of enemy that stands in the way of a balanced rhythm in our lives. Moses told Jethro he was operating in the way he was "Because the people want me." Have you ever fallen into that trap? Your spouse or a good friend will ask you why you have to be the one to carry all the responsibilities. Then you respond that it is your job, as if the world will end if you don't do everything put in front of you. The lie is that you're the only person who can do something, and that lie is a rhythm killer.

The ways you think about pace, rhythm, and time management affect how you manage demands, opportunities, and responsibilities. Your own success and influence will suffer without the right mindset, not to mention your health, lifespan, family life, and friendships.

GUIDED SELF-EXAMINATION

1. Do you feel burned out, tired, or stressed? Do you sometimes fantasize about running away from your current circumstances? Do you feel trapped by your responsibilities and see no way out? If so, describe some of these feelings.

_____

_____

_____

_____

_____

_____

_____

_____

_____

_____

_____

2. Place a number next to each of these in order of the priority currently reflected in your life:

_____ Spouse
_____ Family
_____ Work/Ministry
_____ Hobbies
_____ Something else _____

3. What should be their order of priority?

_____ Spouse
_____ Family
_____ Work/Ministry
_____ Hobbies
_____ Something else _____

4. Why did you give these orders of priority?

_____

_____

_____

_____

_____

_____

Live your life in a godly rhythm.

_____

_____

_____

_____

5. Divide your major responsibilities and interests into two categories.

• Responsibilities—those things you must do.

_____

_____

_____

_____

_____

• Interests—those things you enjoy and are life-giving.

_____

_____

_____

_____

_____

_____

6. List the 3 to 5 things that cause you the most stress.

_____

_____

_____

_____

_____

_____

_____

7. What does your sabbath look like for you? Do you practice a regular day of rest? If not, why don't you?

_____

_____

_____

_____

_____

_____

_____

8. What specific steps could you take to restore a godly rhythm to your life?

_____

_____

_____

_____

_____

_____

_____

FOCUSED PRAYER PROMPTS

Here are some prayer prompts to help you as you apply this lesson to your life:

- Father, help me to know and follow Your priorities. I want them to drive my responsibilities.

_____

_____

_____

_____

_____

_____

_____

_____

- Lord, show me those things I need to pause until another season.

_____

_____

_____

_____

_____

_____

_____

- Holy Spirit, reveal to me the lie I have believed that derails godly rhythm in my life.

_____

_____

_____

_____

_____

_____

Live your life in a godly rhythm.

_____

_____

- Lord, show me what only I can do and what I should delegate.

_____

_____

_____

_____

_____

_____

- Spirit, show me what I should let go so my life can come into a godly rhythm.

_____

_____

_____

_____

_____

_____

Lesson 11

Seek and embrace what is true.

WOULD YOU CALL yourself a "learner"? Do you think of yourself as a humble person? Can you receive correction with an open mind and heart? Or are you self-willed and stubborn? Would people describe you as someone who is "difficult to lead"? How do you handle coaching when someone is trying to help you improve? How you answer these questions will give you a fairly good understanding of your character. Your answers are strong indicators of whether you will seek and embrace what is true or not.

How much do you know about ostriches? They're really very interesting birds. Ostriches can look quite foolish. For example, they're large, flightless birds with long legs and necks, all sticking out of a round body. However, those thin legs can propel them to great speed with remarkable ability to maneuver. They hit speeds up to 40 miles per hour for a sustained period of time. Their legs deliver such a powerful kick that when cornered they can use them to kill or injure an enemy. Contrary to a popular myth, ostriches don't bury their heads in sand when threatened, but they will lie down with their heads against the ground making it appear as though their heads are buried to hide from danger. When confronted with danger, their preference is to run or hide rather than fight.

Some people approach the danger much in the same way ostriches do. They hide or deny it, or they run away and avoid it. They want positive encounters, and fear those that are negative. Rather than confronting error and embracing truth, they will flee from it, only to do the hard work of confronting problems as a last resort. How do you respond to those dangerous relational encounters that arise in your life? When confronted, do you prefer to run or live close to the ground in hiding? What is the usual way you handle uncomfortable truth?

Consider the following three examples of individuals from the Bible. How did they respond to truth? Did they pursue and embrace it? Or did they run and hide from it?

- King Solomon was a wise person. In fact, the Bible says he was the wisest person to have ever lived. What do wise people do? They embrace truth and live in the light of God's Word. At the age of twelve, Solomon responded to God's offer of a "blank check" by asking God to give him wisdom and a heart to know the difference between good and evil. Later in life, Solomon's ungodly wives turned him and the kingdom away from the light of God's Word, but the great successes he knew in life came from seeking and embracing God's truth.
- Samson the judge was graciously given God's favor. However, he didn't seem to understand that none of us are permanently guaranteed favor or blessing regardless of our actions. If we ever stop seeking what is true and embracing it, then we will find ourselves yielding to foolish thoughts and actions with disastrous results. Samson is an example of a foolish person. Foolish people may be very bright and gifted, but they are difficult to lead. God gave him amazing strength. Samson was smart and creative. His strength made him dominant and influential, even over his Philistine enemies. As a judge, he brought about justice for the people of Israel, but at what cost? Samson's attitudes and actions were foolish, and he

was a relationally difficult person. Foolish people resist input and deny the impact of their actions. Samson required strong correction from the Lord because he would not seek and embrace what was true. From Samson, we learn that painful is the path of foolishness, but brokenness can bring about restoration. Through our humility, God can fulfill His purposes in our lives regardless of our past foolishness (see Judges 13).

- Ahab is a biblical example of an evil person. An evil person wants their own way and resists truth by denying truth and pointing fingers of blame through accusation, resistance, and stonewalling. These were qualities that characterized Ahab's life. He did not seek God but defaulted to his own desires and resisted rather than embraced truth. The lesson from Ahab's life is simple: Bad company will turn our seeking into the pursuit of our selfish desires and keep us from embracing truth from any source (see 1 Kings 16:30).

GUIDED SELF-EXAMINATION

1. Are you seeking truth in every area of your life? How do you seek to know God's will and do it? Are there times when you stubbornly go your own way? Are you keeping company with people who are godless and self-willed, while still thinking you can enjoy their way of life without being spiritually affected by it? Why have you responded to each of these questions in the way you did?

_____

_____

_____

_____

_____

_____

_____

_____

2. What would you say are the five most prominent qualities that characterize your life?

_____

_____

_____

_____

_____

_____

_____

3. How do you typically respond to conflict? Do you run? Do you
   hide? Or do you confront the problem and work through it?

_____

_____

_____

_____

_____

_____

_____

4. Have you seen examples of people being wise, foolish, or
   evil? Give examples of each of these types of behavior. Which
   one most exemplifies you and why?

_____

_____

_____

_____

_____

_____

_____

_____

_____

_____

FOCUSED PRAYER PROMPTS

Here are some prayer prompts to help you as you apply this lesson to your life:

- Lord Jesus, I ask You to mold me and develop me more into Your image and according to Your character.

_____

_____

_____

_____

_____

_____

- Holy Spirit, give me the courage to confront the difficult issues and conflicts I have to face every day.

_____

_____

Seek and embrace what is true.

_____

_____

_____

_____

_____

- Father, teach me and shape me into a person who embraces learning. I want to know more about You every day.

_____

_____

_____

_____

_____

_____

- Lord God, help me to live as a wise person. I want Your wisdom to fill me completely.

_____

_____

_____

_____

_____

_____

_____

_____

Lesson 12

Be nice to people who are different.

How do you treat others? Do you treat everyone with the same amount of respect? If someone is rude or unkind to you, do you respond to them in the same way? Or are you gentle and kind toward the people to whom you can relate but intemperate and impatient with those who are "different"?

It amazes me that others are always observing my responses to people and situations. I'm often not even aware they are watching my interactions. With the prevalence of social media and cell phone cameras, none of us can live completely anonymous lives "off the grid," unless we actually move out into the wilderness. We are mere moments away from becoming famous or infamous for how we behave in public or by what we post on social media. Since you know this kind of exposure is very possible and real, it should not be the only reason you are nice to others, but it should be a stark reminder to guard your words, actions, and interactions. This is wise advice the apostle Paul gave to the believers in Ephesus: "Let no corrupting talk come out of your mouths, but only such as is good for building up, as fits the occasion, that it may give grace to those who hear" (Ephesians 4:29).

First, remember *kindness always wins the day*. As believers, we don't respond to bad behavior with an equal measure of our own vibrato and ill treatment. The Bible tells us to give gentle responses, because they turn away wrath (Proverbs 15:1). Yes, people can be difficult and different, and sometimes they can even be "weird." At other times, they will be downright rude. Can we give any of those as a justification to treat people poorly or even reject them? Are we allowed to ignore them, write them off, answer with our own rude response, or even something more drastic?

Jesus sent some of His disciples to Samaria as advance men to make preparations for His visit there, but the people were neither welcoming nor nice. Instead, they rudely rejected the disciples and Jesus for the simple reason that He was on His way to Jerusalem. When the brothers James and John witnessed the Samaritan's response, they boldly asked Jesus if He wanted them to call fire down from heaven to consume those Samaritans. They felt righteously justified in their request. Of course, why wouldn't it be appropriate to ask God to wipe out those rude Samaritans? But Jesus would have none of it. Rather He rebuked James and John for their response. When Jesus gave them the nickname *Boanerges* ('sons of thunder'), it was not a compliment! Some manuscripts say that He told them, "You do not know what manner of spirit you are of, for the son of man came not to destroy people's lives but to save them" (see Luke 9:51–56).

Second, *retaliation is never the right response.* Jesus' followers don't have an excuse to retaliate because of someone's rudeness. Jesus told us to treat people like we want to be treated (Matthew 7:12). I know this is especially hard when people are mean, but it is what we are called to do.

The Jewish religious leaders constantly found offense with Jesus because He kept company and ate with sinners, including tax collectors and prostitutes. They expected Him to shun sinners in the same way they did to prevent becoming defiled by their sin. When the leaders confronted Jesus about His habits, He told them that it was not the healthy who needed a doctor but those who were sick. Then He went on to say that He came *not* to call the righteous but sinners (Mark 2:17). Jesus refused to stay away from people who were different or out of the social mainstream.

Third, *we must become steadfast in our convictions*. As mature believers, and especially leaders in the body of Christ, we must be strong enough in our character and convictions to be around people who don't hold our same values. We must not be influenced to change because of any pressure they might put on us. God expects you to become the influence rather than the one who is influenced!

You must become adept at practicing the following three responses as you encounter people who are different from you:

1. *Recognize* when you are resisting someone because they are different.
2. *Push* through your fear and discomfort with their difference.
3. *Act* with grace in response to the differences of others and seek to understand them.

GUIDED SELF-EXAMINATION

1. Ask yourself this hard question: *Am I rejecting someone around me because they are different from me?* Or has someone upset you because of the way they treated you? Have you retaliated with your responses, either directly or passive-aggressively because of the way someone treated you?

_____

_____

_____

_____

_____

_____

_____

_____

_____

2. Who are some people you feel are weird because they are different? You may use initials to protect identities.

_____

_____

_____

_____

_____

_____

_____

3. Have you been mistreated in the past because you were different from others? Explain.

_____

_____

Be nice to people who are different.

_____

_____

_____

_____

_____

_____

4. What are some ways that you have retaliated when you have experienced unkind and rude behavior?

_____

_____

_____

_____

_____

_____

_____

5. In the 3 responses previously mentioned, which is the most difficult for you to do? Recognize your resistance? Push through discomfort? Or act with grace?

_____

_____

_____

_____

_____

_____

_____

_____

FOCUSED PRAYER PROMPTS

Here are some prayer prompts to help you as you apply this lesson to your life:

- Lord Jesus, let Your kindness and grace be reflected in my life.

_____

_____

_____

_____

_____

_____

_____

Be nice to people who are different.

- I am asking for Your help so I can accept and bless these specific people who are different than me. (You may use initials.) Even when I cannot completely understand them, I want Your mind and heart to be my mind and heart.

_____

_____

_____

_____

_____

_____

_____

- Lord, I need to forgive these people because I have been hurt by them when they have not treated me well because I am different from them. (You may use initials.)

_____

_____

_____

_____

_____

_____

Lesson 13

You are either an influence or you are being influenced.

YOU KNOW THE term "peer pressure." It is often used to describe the *social pressure* we experience from our peer groups, including our friends, associates, family members, and other people close to us. These groups of people have the ability, proximity, and your respect, so they can often influence you to take certain actions, adopt certain values, or otherwise conform your thoughts and behaviors to theirs in order to be accepted.

We often think of teenagers when we talk about peer pressure, but that would be a mistake to think only teens can experience it. Unfortunately, no one is immune to this pressure, and we never really grow out of it. Our age or level of spiritual maturity doesn't make it disappear. You see, God created us to live in relationships with others. What people think of us and whether they accept us or not really is important to each of us. We often experience the tension between relating to others in a way that they find acceptable and holding true to our values regardless of their approval.

God intended for our parents, grandparents, and other family members to form the safety net that would support, protect, and strengthen godly values in our lives. Then those values should be reinforced and supported by our friends and other associates we allow into our inner circle. When we allow people with different values into that circle, we risk following their influence, which may lead us away from our values. God wants us to be influences in all our relationships and to remain strong in our convictions, even as we relate to many different people.

The apostle Peter walked closely with Jesus during His earthly ministry. After the resurrection, Peter became one of the leaders of the emerging church. God used him in many miraculous ways to preach the gospel. One day in a vision, God instructed Peter to go with a group to speak to a devout Gentile (non-Jew) named Cornelius and his family. As a Gentile, Cornelius would not be someone with whom Peter would normally associate. But God told Peter to go with the group asking for him to come to Cornelius's house (Acts 10:17) rather than rejecting these people as unclean.

In the process of Peter going and declaring the Good News, Cornelius and his family received Jesus Christ as their Lord and Savior. At first, Peter was shocked because he previously thought salvation was only for Jewish people and not for Gentiles. Peter's new experience changed everything and raised new questions about how to include the new Gentile believers.

Some of us would consider Peter the least likely to fall for peer pressure, especially after the resurrection. However, in Galatians 2:11, while Peter was visiting the Galatians, he ate and fellowshipped with Gentile believers who were uncircumcised, until his fellow apostle James (also a Jew) arrived in town. When James arrived, Peter's behavior changed, and he would neither fellowship nor eat with the Gentile believers. Peter's behavior was influenced by the peer pressure of James and those who came with him. Peter was concerned with how James and the others would react, so he modified his behavior, which then influenced other Jewish believers, including

Barnabas, to withdraw from the Gentile believers. Peter did not recognize the inconsistency of his actions until Paul confronted his hypocrisy.

In order to receive their acceptance and approval, some people try to pressure us to change how we act or talk, even though they know it is in opposition to our core beliefs. You may encounter a professor or a boss who will shame you in an effort to keep you quiet about your convictions. Sometimes a group of friends will entice you, behaving in a way you know is inconsistent with your understanding of right and wrong. Whether you are pressured to remain silent and inactive or to act and speak in ways you know are wrong, peer pressure is a powerful force you must recognize and manage.

GUIDED SELF-EXAMINATION

1. In what ways have you been influenced to think about and do things that are inconsistent with your convictions? Are you experiencing that kind of pressure right now? Explain.

_____

_____

_____

_____

_____

_____

_____

_____

_____

_____

_____

2. How are you influencing your family, friends, and associates to act in ways that are consistent with their beliefs?

_____

_____

_____

_____

_____

_____

_____

_____

_____

3. How can you encourage others to consider their behavior when it goes against what is right and good?

_____

_____

_____

You are either an influence or you are being influenced.

_____

_____

_____

_____

_____

4. List the 5 family members, friends, or associates who have the most influence in your life. How does each person influence you?

_____

_____

_____

_____

_____

_____

_____

_____

_____

_____

_____

_____

5. List 5 people on whom you have influence. How do you influence them?

_____

_____

_____

_____

_____

_____

_____

_____

_____

_____

6. Describe a time when someone positively influenced you. Describe a time when you were wrongly influenced. How did you respond each time?

_____

_____

_____

_____

You are either an influence or you are being influenced.

_____

_____

_____

_____

_____

_____

_____

PRAYER PROMPTS

Here are some prayer prompts to help you as you apply this lesson to your life:

- Holy Spirit, make me aware of my influence on others.

_____

_____

_____

_____

_____

_____

_____

- Help me to see how others are pressuring me to act in ways I know I shouldn't. Give me the strength and ability to be an influencer rather than one who is influenced.

_____

_____

_____

_____

_____

_____

_____

- Lord Jesus, I want my character to reflect Your grace and consistency as I relate to others.

_____

_____

_____

_____

_____

_____

_____

You are either an influence or you are being influenced.

- Lord, free me from the fear of other people. I want to fear You alone. Guide me in the relationships I have so I will always remain true to You.

Lesson 14

Make spiritual hygiene as important as physical hygiene.

BODY ODOR AND bad breath are unpleasant; that is all there is to it. Messy and unkempt hair can also be a turnoff. Worn, wrinkled, and unwashed clothing and unpolished shoes present an image to others about how much we care about ourselves. Most of us do care. According to the Bureau of Labor and Statistics, the average American family spends about $60 per month, or $700 per year, on personal care products. We are willing to spend that much money so we can look and smell better as we present ourselves to others. Personally, I think that amount may be a little low, but it does reflect the priority we put on our appearance and hygiene.

Just as our personal hygiene is important, so is our spiritual hygiene. In fact, it is more important. When our spiritual hygiene is out of sorts, we are prideful, arrogant, and difficult to get along with in our relationships. It's unattractive and it stinks. People see and smell the spiritual effect of our attitudes, and they know it reflects the condition of our hearts.

Our spiritual lives do give off an aroma to God and others. King David wrote about our prayers, saying they are like an incense, and when we lift our hands it is like an evening sacrifice (Psalm 141:2). In Romans 12:1, the apostle Paul told us that we are to present ourselves as living sacrifices, holy and acceptable to God, which is our reasonable act of worship. Paul also told the Corinthian believers that "whether you eat or drink, or whatever you do, do all to the glory of God. Give no offense . . . Be imitators of me, as I am of Christ" (1 Corinthians 10:31–11:1).

The only way for us to be spiritually attractive and have the aroma of Christ is for us to practice spiritual hygiene. Our spiritual breath must carry the scent of God's breath and Word. Life and death are in the power of our tongues, so we must realize it and allow them to be influenced by our time with God and His Word (see Proverbs 18:21). If we are going to be imitators of Christ, then we must walk with Him every day. In Titus 3:3–6, Paul told us that we are not acceptable to God because of our righteous acts, but we are made acceptable by the washing of regeneration and the renewing of the Holy Spirit. We need the Holy Spirit's work to renew us and to wash from us the deadening influence of the world around us. No matter how hard we work to be acceptable to God, it will take His washing of regeneration and the renewing work of the Holy Spirit. This is the true essence of spiritual hygiene.

Just as we build a routine for our physical hygiene, we must also build a routine and make a place for spiritual hygiene. Physical hygiene takes disciplined effort, but so does spiritual hygiene. Spiritual hygiene comes about through practices like prayer, quiet time with God, reading the Bible, memorizing Scripture, and by personal denial. These disciplines allow us to press into God so we can receive His direction and correction. You will not receive spiritual hygiene by religious practices alone that are done in rote repetition, as they result in acts that reflect a heart of surrender. Only then will you remove wrong attitudes, positively change your behaviors, cleanse your thoughts and words, and restore broken relationships.

GUIDED SELF-EXAMINATION

Are you actively practicing spiritual hygiene? Does your spiritual life have a sweet-smelling aroma? Are you diligently and regularly being washed with regeneration and being renewed by the presence and work of the Holy Spirit?

1. What spiritual hygiene habits do you regularly practice?

_____

_____

_____

_____

_____

_____

_____

2. How do you incorporate prayer regularly into your daily life?

_____

_____

_____

_____

_____

_____

_____

3. Do you regularly listen to podcasts or sermons to challenge you to grow? Which ones? Do you read Christian books? Which ones? What are some of the other intentional ways you work on growing your spiritual life?

_____

_____

_____

_____

_____

_____

_____

_____

_____

FOCUSED PRAYER PROMPTS

Here are some prayer prompts to help you as you apply this lesson to your life:

- Dear Father, show me the areas of my life that need Your cleaning.

_____

_____

_____

_____

_____

_____

_____

- I ask you, Lord Jesus, to give me grace and strength to be consistent with my spiritual hygiene practices.

_____

_____

_____

_____

_____

_____

_____

_____

- Holy Spirit, I ask You to be my partner to walk with me in my spiritual hygiene practices.

_____

_____

_____

_____

_____

_____

_____

Lesson 15

Life is lived in seasons, so learn to recognize and celebrate their coming and going.

KING SOLOMON WROTE that "for everything there is a season, and a time for every matter under heaven" (Ecclesiastes 3:1). Seasons have purpose and a defined duration. They can become wearisome and lead us to become impatient. We find ourselves looking for them to end, which may cause us to short circuit their intended purpose as we take untimely actions. In the process, sometimes the result is that we extend their duration.

Our lives have seasons and can be divided into roughly seven-year developmental cycles. Ecclesiastes tells us that God has laid out our lives in ten developmental seasons (or 70 years). If we are afforded additional seasons beyond ten, they are by "reason of strength" (or our own contributions to good health) and God's blessing. When we are young, we think the seasons of our life will never end. As we get older, however, we realize how quickly these seasons go by and wish we could replay some of them for greater effectiveness.

When we are in circumstances that are pleasant and enjoyable, we hope they will never end. But when we are in a season with difficult circumstances that test our character, try our patience, and bring pain, we will plead and beg for that season to end, and end "Now!" The purpose of the circumstances we face in these seasons is to train, test, or prepare us, or to use us to impact particular people or situations. Depending on how well we navigate the circumstances of these seasons, we may find we repeat them by taking one more learning lap around a particular circumstance or situation.

You must understand *there is no way to avoid seasons*. God has built them into the rhythm of our lives. If you spend all your time trying to avoid a particular developmental season, then it will not help your overall growth in the long run. Neither will you benefit if you simply try to extract yourself from all the circumstances of a season. If all you do is resist, you will only prolong each learning experience, or you will be blind to the needs you are assigned to meet in the circumstances.

Since God designed the seasons, don't fight them, but instead embrace and learn from them. The enemy wants to get you to react to a season apart from God's leading. The devil will tell you to avoid all the pain required for your development and to extract yourself from the situation. If you don't have God's approval and just try to make things easier on yourself, you will miss an amazing opportunity to grow.

God's full purposes and His miraculous works are released through the process of the seasons. Think about these saints from the Bible and be encouraged:

- Moses' many "lives" and the deliverance of the children of Israel in Egypt
- Daniel and the circumstances that put him in the lion's den
- Shadrach, Meshach, and Abednego in the fiery furnace
- Jonah's wild journey to Nineveh to deliver God's message
- Elijah's confrontations with Ahab and Jezebel and the prophets of Baal

These are but a few examples of the Bible's encouraging accounts of living through seasons.

In addition to developmental seasons and circumstantial seasons, there are also spiritual seasons that we must navigate and even endure as we journey along with God. These seasons, like those on our annual calendar, come and go with intended beneficial spiritual results. They deepen our faith, expand our trust in God, and enable us to identify and discover gifts that have lain dormant. In a spiritual season, you must remind yourself of these biblical truths: *God loves you, He has good plans for you, He will not try to drive you away, nor will He end your life.* The enemy wants you to believe God does not care about you, He does not want good for you, He wants to separate Himself from you, and He wants to destroy you. Do not believe these lies. The devil is trying to drive a wedge between you and God. Refuse to play on the enemy's team and win by letting God bring about His purposes in your life.

GUIDED SELF-REFLECTION

Do you have an awareness of seasons and how they affect your life?

1. Right now, are you experiencing "seasonal fatigue" because of circumstances and situations you are facing? What spiritual season would you say you are in right now?

_____

_____

_____

_____

_____

_____

_____

_____

2. As you look back on your life, can you identify the developmental, circumstantial, and spiritual seasons? If so, list them.

_____

_____

_____

_____

_____

_____

_____

3. How is the season you are currently experiencing impacting your life right now? Why do you think this is so?

_____

_____

_____

_____

_____

_____

_____

_____

_____

4. Tell a story about one of the circumstantial seasons in your life. What did you learn from that experience?

_____

_____

_____

_____

_____

_____

_____

_____

_____

PRAYER PROMPTS

Here are some prayer prompts to help you as you apply this lesson to your life:

- Father, I ask for grace in the seasons of my life. I need it now, and I know I will need it in the future.

_____

_____

_____

_____

_____

_____

_____

- Holy Spirit, I need understanding that can only come from You. Help me to see what You are trying to teach me in this circumstantial season. I need You to help me discern so I will know and do Your will.

_____

_____

_____

_____

_____

_____

_____

_____

- Lord Jesus, I need Your love to help me move beyond the fatigue I sometimes feel. Only You can renew me, and I submit my heart to You for that purpose.

_____

_____

_____

_____

_____

_____

_____

Lesson 16

Don't take up an offense, especially one that is not your own.

KING SOLOMON WROTE,

> Iron sharpens iron,
>   and one man sharpens another (Proverbs 27:17).

Consider the process Solomon describes in this proverb as it relates to both friendship and accountability. In Solomon's day, one iron blade rubbed or struck against another blade to sharpen it. In the process, both tools became more effective. This biblical illustration uses a common practice to give insight into our human interactions.

Each person has a distinct set of experiences and a unique personality. While we have similarities, those different gifts, experiences, and perspectives create relational challenges. As we interact with others, we experience pressure that can lead to positive change. In the Christian community, God intends this process to make us better, to clarify our strengths, and to prepare us for His purposes and assignments.

However, the pressure created by these interactions may also inflict pain, cause hurt, or produce an unjust or undeserved result. These interactions can be difficult to navigate, so we often look to others for their support and perspectives. You may find that a friend, colleague, or family member will call on you with their pain or feelings of unjust treatment. Navigate these interactions carefully. Don't allow yourself to be pushed past the boundary of care and support. You will know that you are in danger of crossing that line when you join them in their heart struggles and become enmeshed in their pain. Don't wrongly assume that you are helping others by picking up their hurts and pains and becoming offended on behalf of them. Especially don't become a champion of their causes and try to restore justice through revenge or retaliation.

One day, as Jesus was ministering in a crowd, someone called out to him saying, "'Teacher, tell my brother to divide the inheritance with me.' But he said to him, 'Man, who made me a judge or arbitrator over you?'" (Luke 12:13–14). Jesus refused to get involved with the man's offense against his brother.

The prophet Isaiah instructed us to

> "learn to do good;
> seek justice,
>   correct oppression;
> bring justice to the fatherless,
>   plead the widow's cause" (Isaiah 1:17).

This verse encourages us not to stand on the sideline when we see wrong, ignoring what we see is happening. However, we are also not told to take up offenses and so become avengers through retaliation.

We are to respond with encouragement for others to anchor their faith in God's redeeming work and His heart of justice. We are to inspire them to forgive and trust, but not to retaliate. Urge others to follow the paths of justice, and to the extent you have power or influence, correct the oppression and injustice for those you love, especially the fatherless and widow.

If you become angered by what you see, then use that anger to serve God's purpose. Give righteous support and godly counsel, but encourage those who feel they have been wronged to trust God. Don't allow your anger to lead you to sin, especially not by taking up an injustice as your own offense or by planning or participating in retaliation.

GUIDED SELF-REFLECTION

1. Have you become offended by an injustice inflicted on someone else? Have you taken up their offense and joined their desire for retaliation? Explain the situation.

_____

_____

_____

_____

_____

_____

_____

_____

_____

2. How are you sharpening a friend, family member, or colleague with greater faith, courage, and trust in God through your counsel?

_____

_____

_____

_____

_____

_____

_____

_____

3. Do you have a family member or friend who has been treated unjustly and is carrying that hurt today? List those you know who are in this situation along with the pain you see each person has attached to the offense.

_____

_____

_____

_____

Don't take up an offense, especially one that is not your own.

_____

_____

_____

_____

_____

4. Have you been offended by a situation that did not directly affect you, but it has greatly affected someone close to you? Describe that person's offense and how you have also responded to it.

_____

_____

_____

_____

_____

_____

_____

_____

_____

5. Have you ever encouraged retaliation or participated in plans to retaliate? In what way have you become complicit in that kind of reaction?

_____

_____

_____

_____

_____

_____

_____

_____

_____

6. What specific things do you need to do to impart courage in these kinds of situations? How can you help others build faith and strengthen their trust in God?

_____

_____

_____

_____

_____

_____

Don't take up an offense, especially one that is not your own.

_____

_____

_____

_____

FOCUSED PRAYER PROMPTS

Here are some prayer prompts to help you as you apply this lesson to your life:

- Lord, I lift up to You those who are close to me, especially those I know are hurting because they have experienced injustice.

_____

_____

_____

_____

_____

_____

_____

_____

- Holy Spirit, I ask You for wisdom so I will know when I should come to the aid of others. Keep me from taking offense on their behalf.

_____

_____

_____

_____

_____

_____

_____

- Lord Jesus, as You forgave those who did wrong to You, give me the desire to forgive those who have caused pain to the people I love.

_____

_____

_____

_____

_____

_____

_____

Don't take up an offense, especially one that is not your own.

- Father, I know You are a God of justice. Keep me from sin and deliver me from the desire for retaliation and vengeance. I bring my concerns to You, knowing You alone can bring about perfect justice and perfect love.

_____

_____

_____

_____

_____

_____

_____

Lesson 17

Respect and appreciate the platform you have been given.

WHAT IS THE purpose of the platform of influence you are now occupying? Is it to make you happy? Do you think it might be to make others jealous? Or is it for your personal use and benefit? Do you think you produced the platform, or did God have something to do with it? The reality is God wants to showcase us for the world to see and emulate so they will desire to have a relationship with Him. The Bible says, "And all the peoples of the earth shall see that you are called by the name of the LORD, and they shall be afraid of you. And the LORD will make you abound in prosperity" (Deuteronomy 28:10–11a). Our responsibility is to make God our priority, and as we do, He will give us the right platform of influence to showcase His work in us.

The size of our influence is made up of several factors. Character and integrity form the foundation upon which influence is built and determine its ultimate size and long-term scope. Character and integrity give our influence "sticking" power because they affect the ability of others to trust us. In this way, our success is directly related to our character, integrity, and trustworthiness. Out of this foundation, we form our reputation, which is the outward expression of our influence.

As we succeed in our efforts, the scope of our influence will increase. This increase will be followed by wealth, because others will recognize your value and secure your platform of influence. With an increased platform of influence comes an increase of wealth. Wealth will not damage or endanger your influence if it came because of your character and integrity. The Bible tells us that it is God who gives us power to get wealth (see Deuteronomy 8:18). We are also given the truth that when our wealth is built on God's foundation, it is a blessing and does not come with sorrow or a curse (Proverbs 10:22).

In our current society, probably all of us know of platforms of influence that were built on unstable foundations. When influence is disconnected from the foundation of character and integrity, some individuals will manipulate, mislead, and lie to people so they can grow their platform. As they try and influence people to be like them, buy products from them, or believe in the God (or god) they proclaim, we can see they are presenting a false picture of who they are, or even worse, they are using people even while they attempt to influence them. If you do not want to follow those who construct these kinds of platforms of influence, make sure you are always building on the right foundation.

An inheritance is a gift of resources given to you by your parents or grandparents (or spiritual parents) for the purpose of enhancing your influence (Proverbs 13:22). The heritage passed on to us from our parents and grandparents reflects the values, traditions, and the heroes celebrated by them. We do not build our platforms of influence by ourselves. Our families have already established and shaped the foundation, but we enhance it as we build our character, integrity, and trustworthiness. If you alone are responsible for building your influence, then it is also yours to lose. Ultimately God determines the size and scope of your influence, but others contribute to it.

GUIDED SELF-REFLECTION

1. Are you aware that you have a platform of influence, even if you think it is small today? How are you building that platform?

_____

_____

_____

_____

_____

_____

_____

2. Have you thought you alone were responsible for your influence? Who else has helped you build it?

_____

_____

_____

_____

_____

_____

_____

_____

3. Are you content with your current platform of influence? Why or why not?

_____

_____

_____

_____

_____

_____

_____

_____

4. Do you consider yourself a person of character, integrity, and trustworthiness? What kind of reputation do you have with family, neighbors, and business associates?

_____

_____

Respect and appreciate the platform you have been given.

_____

_____

_____

_____

_____

_____

_____

5. Describe a situation where you became aware of your
   influence and its impact.

_____

_____

_____

_____

_____

_____

_____

_____

_____

6. When you think of these foundation ingredients (character, integrity, and trustworthiness), which one do you think is your weakest?

_____

_____

_____

_____

_____

_____

_____

7. What are you known for? That would be a simple way to describe your reputation.

_____

_____

_____

_____

_____

_____

_____

8. What resources have you inherited that are part of your influence? Does the heritage passed from your parents and grandparents (or someone else) give you a secure foundation for influence? Describe these resources and your heritage.

FOCUSED PRAYER PROMPTS

Here are some prayer prompts to help you as you apply this lesson to your life:

- Lord, I want to have character, integrity, and trustworthiness so that my influence will grow for Your glory.

_____

_____

_____

_____

_____

_____

_____

_____

- Holy Spirit, give me spiritual eyes to see opportunities for influence that are in Your path today.

_____

_____

_____

_____

_____

Respect and appreciate the platform you have been given.

_____

_____

_____

- God, I want my reputation and influence to extend beyond me to the generations. I ask You to guide me in Your paths.

_____

_____

_____

_____

_____

_____

_____

Lesson 18

Love is courageous, yet does not enable.

HOW IS LOVE expressed in your life? How about in your family? Some people would define the goal of love as the absence of conflict. Still others would say that love is a feeling of compassionate care that leads to attraction and results in commitment. If feelings are the foundation of love, then what do you do when the feeling wanes or even disappears? Attraction and commitment can also leave. How, then, do we define love in the way we treat others and relate to them, especially those closest to us? Jesus said we will show people we are His disciples by the way we love others (John 13:35).

The apostle Paul says,

> Love is patient and kind; love does not envy or boast; it is not arrogant or rude. It does not insist on its own way; it is not irritable or resentful; it does not rejoice at wrongdoing, but rejoices with the truth. Love bears all things, believes all things, hopes all things, endures all things (1 Corinthians 13:4–7).

It takes courage to be truthful in the face of conflict and at the potential of rejection. It also takes courage to engage and participate in building and growing a relationship that does not control, manipulate, or use another person for your own personal benefit. And it takes courage to confront situations rather than excuse them. In courage, we humble ourselves in surrender and accountability to another person.

If your definition of love includes "never having to say you're sorry," then you don't have a biblical perspective of love. If you think love means that you must totally and completely accept everything about a person regardless of their behavior, then you have misunderstood the Bible here as well. Any definition of love that doesn't allow you to confront problems, but requires you to overlook problems, is not God's perspective. If a person engages in brash and domineering behaviors, if they invalidate your perspectives, if they make self-centered demands, or if they are just unkind in their actions, then they are not following God's way of love. Any relationship that enables narcissistic behaviors from another person, or one that does not allow and accept reasonable boundaries, is unhealthy rather than truly loving.

Even with all of these reminders, we must recognize that every person is a work in progress; we should especially know this about ourselves. Many of us have been bruised and damaged as we have journeyed through life. When we recognize this reality, it will lead us to be more gracious and patient toward each other. In relationships, we partner with others to grow, serve, and walk through life. Successful partnerships must reflect a tension between honest communication and gracious understanding. These partnerships include mutual respect that would never intentionally use or abuse another person for our own personal gains. It also means that at times we must stand our ground and insist that others respect our emotional and physical boundaries, even when others try to violate them in the name of "love."

These lessons are difficult to apply on our own. It is good for us to realize that God never intended us to love apart from His work and presence in our lives. His intention from the

Love is courageous, yet does not enable.

very beginning was to form a three-stranded partnership with two individuals and Himself. It was Adam, Eve, and God in a relational partnership in the Garden of Eden (Genesis 3:8). In all of our relationships, God does not intend for us to navigate alone. His presence gives us the power to love.

GUIDED SELF-REFLECTION

1. In relationships, would you say you dominate or enable? Explain.

_____

_____

_____

_____

_____

_____

_____

_____

2. Are you courageous in confronting unhealthy tendencies in your relationships? Explain.

_____

_____

_____

_____

_____

_____

_____

_____

_____

3. How does your relationship with God influence the way you
relate to the people you love?

_____

_____

_____

_____

_____

_____

_____

_____

_____

4. Write your own definition of love, and then describe how you reflect love in your closest relationships.

_____

_____

_____

_____

_____

_____

_____

_____

_____

_____

5. Describe a relationship in which you have found it difficult to demonstrate love.

_____

_____

_____

_____

_____

_____

_____

_____

6. Describe a situation where you acted with courage to confront a person who breached a boundary, engaged in unhealthy behavior, or acted in a domineering way.

_____

_____

_____

_____

_____

_____

_____

_____

_____

7. Describe the behavior of someone you know who needs to change their definition of love.

_____

_____

Love is courageous, yet does not enable.

_____

_____

_____

_____

_____

_____

_____

FOCUSED PRAYER PROMPTS

Here are some prayer prompts to help you as you apply this lesson to your life:

- Lord Jesus, show me how to love someone who I am struggling to love.

_____

_____

_____

_____

_____

_____

- Lord, give me courage and wisdom to confront that difficult situation that has me tied in knots.

_____

_____

_____

_____

_____

_____

_____

- Lord, I need strength to set boundaries with someone I care about who is damaging in the way they express love.

_____

_____

_____

_____

_____

_____

_____

Lesson 19

Be gracious in transition and remember God is in charge!

TRANSITION IS THE term we use to describe the time required and the processes necessary to produce change in our lives. Change is a fact of life. Things that grow also change. Transition brings about a new state of being. Since none of us are immune to change, all of us will experience transition multiple times in our life, whether at work, in our marriages, or in our personal lives.

Only God does not change, and in His sovereignty, He knows all things. I don't think God views change as good or bad. In fact, Scripture presents change as part of the process of life. We are told to love the Lord with our whole hearts and not to count on our own understanding. Only then will God lead us on a straight path to His purposes in our lives (see Proverbs 3:5–6). The apostle Paul wrote that God causes all things to work together for our good if we are committed to His purposes (see Romans 8:28).

So, when you are faced with transition, don't be too hard on yourself. You are on life's journey. Your purpose is to know God and do His will in all circumstances. Ask Him to show you the way. You will experience many different types of transitions. Regardless of the kind of transition, the cause of the transition will not ultimately define you, since only your response to God and His sovereign work will make the final declaration of "good" or "bad."

THREE TYPES OF TRANSITION

Consider these three types of transition:

1. TRANSITION BY CHOICE

Sometimes we can be led to change through our own choosing. Maybe the choice is a job promotion or a career change with greater opportunities. It might be a choice to leave an unhealthy relationship. We usually view these changes as positive at the time they are made. However, only time will reveal if our choices have good long-term effects or if they further God's purposes in our lives.

2. TRANSITION BY FAULT

Change also comes about sometimes because of a mistake, an oversight, a misjudgment, or participation in illegal or immoral activities. These transitions can be accompanied by shame, regret, embarrassment, and possibly punishment. The negative emotions associated with this type of transition lead us to conclude they are bad. They may be devastating to the point of no recovery when fear and self-pity set in. As with any transition, only time will tell if the changes bring about positive or negative effects. A person may not only be impacted by the initial mistake, but also by the reactions to the results.

3. TRANSITION OUTSIDE YOUR CONTROL

Finally, change can happen because of unforeseen circumstances that are outside of our control. These circumstances include business closures, loss of a job, the unexpected death of a loved one, or a medical issue that alters your or someone else's life. These transitions are often a surprise and usher in a season of grief that leaves us disoriented as we struggle to cope and find hope. This type of transition, like the others, requires time to process, adjust, and move forward. Our initial responses might be shock, fear, disorientation, or hopelessness. We might even conclude that no good will come of this situation and we will never recover, but time will tell. Like the other types of transition, our reactions have a great influence on the final results.

FIVE WAYS TO LEARN FROM TRANSITION

If someone around you is experiencing transition, remember everyone faces changes in life, so be gracious. Help people going through these changes to understand the different types of transition. Also, encourage them in these five ways so they can learn from their transitions and move forward with God.

1. Build their faith.
2. Help them to overcome shame, regret, and embarrassment.
3. Remind them that God is sovereign and in control of all our circumstances.
4. If they are walking through pain associated with their transitions, then be compassionate.
5. Help them to anchor their trust in God.

GUIDE SELF-EXAMINATION

1. Are you in transition right now, or have you been recently? If so, what type of transition is it or was it?

_____

_____

_____

_____

_____

_____

_____

2. Are you resisting change in some area of your life? If so, describe it.

_____

_____

_____

_____

_____

Be gracious in transition and remember God is in charge!

_____

_____

_____

_____

_____

3. Have you been harsh and judgmental with someone in transition? If so, how will you respond better in the future?

_____

_____

_____

_____

_____

_____

_____

_____

4. List the types of transition you have experienced and provide details for each type.

_____

_____

_____

_____

_____

_____

_____

_____

_____

_____

5. How have you seen good come from a difficult transition?

_____

_____

_____

_____

_____

_____

_____

6. Have you made a transition by choice that did not work out? If so, explain.

_____

_____

_____

_____

_____

_____

_____

_____

_____

7. What has God taught you through transitions in your life?

_____

_____

_____

_____

_____

_____

_____

_____

_____

PRAYER PROMPTS

Here are some prayer prompts to help you as you apply this lesson to your life:

- Lord, show Yourself to me as I go through transitions and changes in my life. I want to know what You are trying to say to me in each situation.

_____

_____

_____

_____

_____

_____

_____

- Holy Spirit, I need Your help to overcome shame, regret, and embarrassment over transitions I have experienced.

_____

_____

Be gracious in transition and remember God is in charge!

_____

_____

_____

_____

_____

- Lord Jesus, I need Your compassion and wisdom to help others as they experience transitions in their lives. I want Your love to be my example and guide.

_____

_____

_____

_____

_____

_____

_____

Lesson 20

Watch your six—at all times!

DO YOU REALIZE we are in a constant spiritual war between good and evil? It is a battle in the heavenly realms between God and Satan, yet it often spills over into our earthly space. Unseen spiritual forces resist the things of God and try to discourage us and rob us of hope. Sometimes these spiritual forces manifest through relational situations we experience with people at work, with our friends, or with family members. Occasionally they will surface in situations with people we don't even know. These forces will even show themselves in attempts to drive us to lust and follow ungodly desires.

We may incorrectly think that our problem is only with other people, but the Bible tells a different story. We are in a battle with spiritual forces that are working to undermine our commitment to love God and serve Him. These demonic enemies want to push us to serve ourselves and put our own interests before God's (see Ephesians 6:12). These adversaries will work through circumstances and tempt us to fulfill our God-given appetites in ways that God doesn't approve (see James 1:14).

We are deceiving ourselves if we think we can easily identify which battles are spiritual and which are not. Are you just having a bad day, or is it the spiritual warfare set against you? All of us struggle with anger, temptations of the flesh, physical limitations, hunger, tiredness, anger, and pride. But are these the only factors that lead us to sin? The answer is *no*. We are all in a pitched spiritual battle, whether we like it or not, or whether we wish to engage in it or not.

I want you to realize, at all times, that you cannot become spiritually complacent. You must be constantly vigilant because you're in a battle, and the enemy is out for your destruction. He is ruthless. Paul told the Ephesians to look circumspectly as they walk through the circumstances of life, not to be unwise, but wise. He encouraged them not be foolish, but to work hard to understand the Lord's will in the hard issues of the moment. When the battle is at its hardest, it's easy for us to search for comfort rather than being diligent in our search for God's movement in a situation. That is why Paul told the Ephesians not to get drunk with wine, meaning they should not medicate their pain and frustration. They were to be sober and ready for battle. In all of these battles, he told them the best course was to be filled with the Holy Spirit (see Ephesians 5:15–21).

Watch your six! I mean watch your back, so the enemy can't sneak up on you. Carefully consider all your relationships and involvements so you won't become compromised and give the enemy an advantage. Walk with humility and depend upon key people the Lord has put around you to fight the battle with you. Never forget that the enemy has you in his sights! But the Holy Spirit has already placed the best weapons in your arsenal.

GUIDED SELF-REFLECTION

1. Where are you engaged in this spiritual battle right now?

_____

_____

_____

_____

_____

_____

_____

_____

2. How are you watching your six?

_____

_____

_____

_____

_____

_____

3. Where is the front line of your spiritual battle today? Is it at work? Is it in your marriage? Is it with a family member or friend?

_____

_____

_____

_____

_____

_____

_____

_____

4. Do you believe a person is being used to engage in battle with you right now?

_____

_____

_____

_____

_____

_____

_____

5. Can you think of a time when you were lulled into complacency in your spiritual battle? Explain.

_____

_____

_____

_____

_____

_____

_____

_____

_____

_____

6. Discuss a spiritual battle that you feel you handled the
   right way.

_____

_____

_____

_____

_____

_____

_____

_____

_____

FOCUSED PRAYER PROMPTS

Here are some prayer prompts to help you as you apply this lesson to your life:

- Holy Spirt, fill me with Your power and authority to face the battle.

_____

_____

_____

_____

_____

_____

_____

- Lord, I lift up the person who is against me in a spiritual battle.

_____

_____

_____

_____

_____

_____

_____

_____

- Spirit, I need Your wisdom and understanding to become like a Navy Seal in fighting and resisting the enemy.

_____

_____

_____

_____

_____

_____

_____

Lesson 21

Finish strong and don't coast to the finish line!

FOR MOST OF my adult life, I have been a runner. I'm not a competitive runner, but I run to stay in good physical shape. I have noticed a few things about the way I approach running. First, before I start, I want to know where the finish line is and the overall length of the course. Is it three miles, four, or even five? How far will I run today? I need a mental picture of the layout of the course so I can monitor my progress.

Second, I want to know the conditions I will encounter. Is it windy? Which way is the wind blowing, since that might determine the direction I am going to run (running with the wind is a lot easier than running into the wind)? Is the temperature hot or cold today (this data lets me know how to dress)? Knowing the conditions helps me prepare mentally for the run.

Then, as I start my run, I have come to realize the first mile is the hardest because it sets the pace for the rest of my run. That initial mile is also when my body fights the hardest against me, trying to convince me that running on this particular day is a bad idea. My body will complain, using my inner conscience to say, "We don't want to run today." If that doesn't get me to quit, then it tries to convince me to stop as I think about the course I am running. I will wonder if I'm going to be able to complete the run. No matter what distance I have chosen, my body will tell me it is too far, and I may die in the process, so I need to stop and rest. If I will push through all these objections that try to get me to quit, or at least to walk and not run, then in the second mile my conscience will begin to align with my body and my will. It's then that I can get down to the business of running rather than resisting it.

Life is like a race we are running. In terms of years, the course is defined as about 70 years, or maybe 80 if we are strong enough. Knowing the length of our race helps us get a mental picture of life. It helps us pace ourselves and evaluate our progress along the way. In the race of life, we can find ourselves in a mental crisis if we realize that our pace has been too fast, and we may begin thinking we will not have what it takes to complete the race. On the other end of the crisis, we may realize that our pace is too slow, or we have gotten off course, and we aren't going to finish the race or end up at the finish line where we thought.

Some of us are fair weather "life-race-runners." If the conditions in our lives are too hot or too cold, if things are too windy or we face a lot of resistance, then we sometimes decide not to run. Rather than evaluate the conditions and prepare accordingly, we stop running and sit on the sidelines. We are stationary, but we remain on the automatic conveyor belt of life, which moves us toward the end of our race with little or no effort on our part. God has set the race of life to operate in this way. He designed us for partnership to pursue our purpose in Him. He won't do all the work for us, nor will He fulfill our purpose without our participation.

No matter where you currently are in life's race (as I said earlier, our race has 10 seven-year segments, or eight or more if by reason of strength—see Psalm 90:10), you are battling the elements on the course or in your head. The elements make up the spiritual battle that is part of your race. No individual race is precisely the same, so don't compare your race or progress with someone else. It is your race to run with God's purpose and in partnership with Him.

The author of Hebrews gives us this encouragement:

Therefore, since we are surrounded by so great a cloud of witnesses, let us also lay aside every weight, and sin which clings so closely, and let us run with endurance the race that is set before us, looking to Jesus, the founder and perfecter of our faith, who for the joy that was set before him endured the cross, despising the shame, and is seated at the right hand of the throne of God (Hebrews 12:1–2).

Stop listening to your inner complaints and push through. Run your race, the whole race, and finish strong!

GUIDED SELF-REFLECTION

1. Do you believe you are running your race, or are you sitting on the sideline? Explain.

_____

_____

_____

_____

_____

_____

_____

_____

_____

2. Where do you think are you in your life's race? Are you in the first mile or the seventh mile? Explain.

_____

_____

_____

_____

_____

_____

_____

_____

3. Do you think your pace is too fast or too slow? Explain.

_____

_____

_____

_____

_____

Finish strong and don't coast to the finish line!

_____

_____

_____

_____

_____

4. What conditions are you encountering in your race that
   make you want to quit?

_____

_____

_____

_____

_____

_____

_____

_____

5. What encouragement do you need today so you can carry on
   with your race and finish strong? Explain.

_____

_____

_____

_____

_____

_____

_____

_____

_____

FOCUSED PRAYER PROMPTS

Here are some prayer prompts to help you as you apply this lesson to your life:

- Dear Father, give me the endurance I need to run my race.

_____

_____

_____

_____

_____

_____

_____

- Holy Spirit, help me to overcome the inner voices that try to get me to quit.

_____

_____

_____

_____

_____

_____

_____

_____

- Lord Jesus, I know You ran the race for me. I ask You to direct my pace so I will have the strength to run hard to the finish line.

_____

_____

_____

_____

_____

_____

_____

_____

About the Author

TOM LANE is the apostolic senior pastor of Gateway Church in the Dallas/Fort Worth Metroplex. He oversees the Outreach Ministries of Gateway Church, which include The Kings University, Gateway Global Ministry, Kingdom Business Leaders, and Gateway Church Network. Tom works with the executive teams in each of these ministry areas to execute the vision and values of the church. Prior to this position, he served as Gateway Church's executive senior pastor for 12 years and as the Dallas campus pastor for two years.

Tom's vocational ministry experience spans more than 37 years. Before joining the staff at Gateway Church, he served at Trinity Fellowship Church in Amarillo, Texas. Tom has experience in a variety of church leadership roles, including business administrator, administrative pastor, executive pastor, and senior pastor.

Tom's extensive ministry expertise and engaging relational style bring a warmth to his speaking, writing, and pastoral ministry. He is the author and co-author of several books, including *Heritage, A Father's Influence to the Generations, Foundations of Healthy Church Government, He Still Speaks, Strong Women and the Men Who Love Them, Conversations with God,* and *Letters from a Dad to a Graduate.*

Tom and his wife, Jan, have been married for over 40 years. They have four married children and 15 grandchildren.

Get the book:

ISBN: 978-1-951227-24-1
www.gatewaypublishing.com

MORE FROM TOM LANE

Foundations of Healthy Church Government

Develop an enduring, biblical model of governance for your church, reignite growth, and move your staff and vision from confusion to unity.

Book: 9781945529306

Heritage: A Father's Influence to the Generations

Tom Lane provides practical tools, biblical foundation, and inspiration for imparting godly character to the generations entrusted to you.

Book: 9781945529399
DVD: 9781949399455

Strong Women and the Men Who Love Them

Using principles and perspectives based in Scripture, couples will learn to appreciate the expression of each person's gifts to benefit the relationship.

Book: 9781629985923
Study Guide: 9781945529771

Printed in Great Britain
by Amazon

56093308R00120